Praise for *Being*

"[A] clear, practical, and powerful approach for navigating through tough times."   —Bonnie Hammer, president,
NBCU Cable Entertainment and Cable Studios

"Unlike most experts in her field, Erika Andersen has an approach to being strategic that's sensible and accessible. With her, you feel capable of creating the business, career, and life you want. She's to strategy what Suze Orman is to personal finance!"   —Nancy Tellem,
senior advisor to the CEO, CBS Corp.

"Over the past decade, in each of the companies I've led, I've relied on Erika Andersen to help me engage my senior team in getting clear about the future we want to create for our enterprise and figuring out what it will take for us to get there. Her vision and strategy process helps us get our heads around complex issues in a way that's unusually simple. I'm always surprised, at the end of a session, how we've made our aspirations practical and built a clear path to achieving them."   —Doug Herzog, president, MTV Networks
Entertainment Group

"My partners and I have turned to Erika Andersen each time our company has reached a new plateau of growth—and generally when we need her expert prodding, analysis, and follow-up to get us over the next organizational hump. When I described our most recent restructuring plan to a friend—a seasoned and successful financial professional—he was certain we must have hired McKinsey & Company to help us think things through. Wrong. It was Erika Andersen."

—Danny Meyer, restaurateur, president,
Union Square Hospitality Group

"To most of us, the thought of articulating a long-term strategy that is both visionary and practical seems an overwhelming task. The approach used by Erika Andersen enables a team to effectively articulate ideas, reach consensus, and formulate a detailed course of action for achieving their vision."

—Kathy Dore, former president,
Canwest Media Broadcasting

"When I became president of Women in Cable Telecommunications in 2001, I realized that the organization needed to reinvent itself. We used the Proteus strategic approach to create a clear, powerful vision of the organization we wanted, and then to continually move toward that vision. Now, in my new role, Proteus is helping us make sure the U.S. track and field team achieves its fullest potential in 2012 and beyond."

—Benita Fitzgerald Moseley,
chief of sport performance, USATF

BEING STRATEGIC

Plan for Success;
Out-think Your Competitors;
Stay Ahead of Change

Erika Andersen

 ST. MARTIN'S GRIFFIN NEW YORK

To my darling Patrick and our FGL

www.stmartins.com

The Library of Congress has cataloged the hardcover edition as follows:

Andersen, Erika.
   Being strategic : plan for success; out-think your competitors; stay ahead of change / Erika Andersen.—1st ed.
       p. cm.
   ISBN 978-0-312-55398-2
   1. Strategic planning.   2. Planning.   I. Title.
   HD30.28.A513 2009
   658.4'012—dc22   2008046037

ISBN 978-0-312-65670-6 (trade paperback)

10   9   8   7   6   5   4

Contents

Acknowledgments   *vii*

Foreword   *ix*

Introduction: If I Hear the Word "Strategic" One More Time, I'll ...   *1*

  1. The Castle on the Hill   *19*

PART ONE
BEING STRATEGIC EVERY DAY

  2. Defining the Challenge: How Can We ... ?   *33*

  3. What Is: Pulling Back the Camera   *45*

  4. What's the Hope: Reasonable Aspiration   *58*

  5. What's in the Way: Facing the Facts   *72*

  6. What's the Path: Roadway First, Then Asphalt   *88*

  7. The Art of Crafting Strategy   *96*

  8. Tactics That Work   *107*

  9. Building on Success   *121*

10. The Castle of You   *138*

CONTENTS

PART TWO
BEING STRATEGIC WITH A GROUP

11. Inviting Others into the Process   *151*

12. Crafting a Strategic Vision   *164*

13. The Art of Facilitation   *210*

14. Strategy as a Way of Life   *247*

15. Castle Building for Fun and Profit   *260*

Acknowledgments

When I began this book, I had no idea how my ability to remain strategic in my own life was going to be tested during this time, and how my life's vision would expand. I could not have done it—personally or professionally—without everyone named on this page:

To the "book team"—Jim Levine, Phil Revzin, Lisa Senz, Barbara Cave Henricks, Dennis Welch, Sara Schneider, and Kerry Evans—for encouraging me to practice what I preach, and for being (each of you) such a wonderful combination of excellence and humor.

To everyone at St. Martin's, for making me feel so welcome.

To all our great clients, for continuing to allow us to help you clarify and move toward your hoped-for future!

To my dear Proteans; I'm glad to know each of you, and I'm so excited about what we're building together.

To Rachel and Ian, Jeff, Kristi, David, Kurt and Anne,

Ann C, Rochelle, and Jan, with my profound gratitude—I wouldn't have made it through the hard times without you.

And to Gjoko—for being exactly who you are.

Foreword

I'm writing this as I'm flying back home to New York, tired but happy; yesterday I taped *Being Strategic with Erika Andersen,* a national pledge drive special for public television, in front of a live audience at Detroit Public Television's beautiful state-of-the-art HD studios. The program begins airing nationally the same month this new paperback edition of the book is released. As you can imagine, I'm thrilled and grateful to have this opportunity to share something that's so important to me with so many people.

When I first began writing *Being Strategic* in 2006, I envisioned this mindset and these skills being made available to many thousands more people than I could ever reach individually. Because I've found this approach to be so helpful—to me, to my clients and colleagues—I wanted to share it as broadly as possible. This capability we call being strategic is like a Swiss Army knife for improving your life: by learning to consistently focus on those core directional choices that will best move you toward your hoped-for future, you can support your success in any area you choose.

And since the hardback edition was published in May of 2009, the future that I (and my marvelous book team) envisioned has begun to unfold in a variety of surprising and exciting ways. The television program brings these skills to everyone in the world who has access to public television—and the DVD of the program offers the additional option of learning the skills whenever and wherever you want.

At the same time, my colleagues at Proteus and I have seen a dramatic increase in client requests for the model and skills of being strategic. We've been using this approach with our clients for twenty years, but over this past year we've conducted the process at even more organizations, from Fortune 50 companies to small private schools; from media companies to manufacturing organizations; from international conglomerates to entrepreneurial start-ups; with long-time clients and brand-new ones. And each group has found the process an extraordinarily simple and powerful way to clarify the future they want to create for themselves and then create a practical roadmap for moving toward that future.

I think part of it is simply serendipitous timing: as the world has begun to emerge from this recent recession, we're seeing that many leaders are approaching the rebuilding of their businesses in a more reflective way: they want to make sure they don't drive back into the same ditch we're just hauling ourselves out of, and they're thinking more deeply about how to create sustainable success for their organizations. The being strategic approach provides a structured way for them to think and decide together with their senior teams about how best to do just that.

We've also noticed individuals thinking in this same way. Having come through these past few difficult years has caused many people to reflect deeply on their lives and careers, and to ask new questions: *How can I find a career that's satisfying and challenging to me? How can I make a positive difference in the world? How can live I live "greener" in significant ways? How can I create a loving relationship that's truly healthy and nourishing?*

And, as you'll find when you read the book you're holding—those *"How can I . . . ?"* questions are the first step on the path to being strategic about your life, in order to create the future that you most desire. . . .

So, however you come to be reading this—whether you picked it up at your local library, borrowed it from a friend, downloaded it onto your e-reader, bought it at your local bookstore, or saw it lying on a park bench and were intrigued by the castle on the cover—I hope you find it engaging and useful in equal measure. I hope this model and these skills become for you a useful tool, that Swiss Army knife you can use to create the business, the career, the life you truly want.

And I'd love to hear about your success! Join the conversation on my blog, at www.thesimplestthing.typepad.com, or e-mail us at connect@proteus-international.com.

Here's to a wonderful future. . . .

Very warmly,
Erika Andersen
April 2010

If I Hear the Word "Strategic" One More Time, I'll . . .

How many times, over the past few months, have you sat in a meeting and heard someone use the word "strategic"? As in: "We're not being very strategic about this" or "We need a strategic plan for project X." And, if your company is like most companies, everyone in the meeting nods wisely, the meeting goes on, and people continue to debate how to approach the situation at hand, with—generally—no one the wiser as to what the speaker actually meant by the word "strategic."

What an odd thing this is, when you think about it. Here's a word that gets used all the time, in a variety of contexts—and people have no common definition for it. That's pretty unusual: whether we're saying "apple" or "sunlight," or something less tangible like "embarrassment" or "realization," there's generally a shared definition. If you ask ten people what "embarrassment" means, you get pretty much the same story.

However, if you were in a meeting where the word "strategic" had just been used and you could magically put little bubbles over people's heads that showed what they were thinking, I'd almost guarantee there wouldn't be much overlap. Let's try it:

The boss says, "We're not being very strategic about this," and her thought bubble says, *Everyone's just focusing on their own department.*

Maybe the CFO thinks, *Yeah, nobody's considering the financial implications.*

And the newly minted MBA in the group thinks, *Right—strategy! Market forces! ROI! Human capital investment!*

The CTO's thought bubble says: *That's for sure—we don't measure anything around here. We just fly by the seat of our pants.*

The COO sighs and thinks, *Oh, great, this means taking months to develop a multi-year strategic plan that will go in a binder and sit on somebody's shelf.*

The VP of Sales is nodding and thinking, *She's right—we need to be MUCH more focused on outsmarting the competition.*

The head of production thinks, *Yeah, nobody around here plans more than about ten minutes ahead.*

Others will say to themselves, *The hell with strategy—I've got deadlines!*

And it's almost a sure bet that at least one person at the meeting will be thinking, *Umm . . . strategy?*

To add to the confusion, if you've read any of the many books available on strategy and strategic thinking, you'll find very little agreement there, either. Some offer principles; some prescribe actions; some promote certain ways of thinking. A great many of the books on strategy talk about it as though it's just an in-depth version of financial modeling or purely focused on the competition. And most of them talk about strategy as though it's something that's only applicable to big, organization-wide decisions. Many describe strategy or strategic thinking as being such a complex undertaking, and so separate from daily action, that you, the reader, immediately say to yourself, *Oh, now I see why companies have strategic planning functions—no one could do this and still have time for their day job!*

OK, SO LET'S JUST STOP SAYING IT, AND MAYBE IT WILL GO AWAY. . . .

Should we all make a solemn pact never to use the word "strategic" again? It's tempting . . . but no. Just because it's ill defined and referred to in confusing and contradictory ways, that doesn't mean "being strategic" isn't an actual (and even a useful) thing. In fact, I'd like to propose to you that there is something both real and important behind all this confusion—that "being strategic" is actually a deeply useful capability, and one that most people can develop.

Being strategic isn't just about making complex long-range

business plans or doing in-depth market analyses (although the ability to think strategically is essential to doing either of those things well). Being strategic—as I'd like to define it here—involves a way of thinking and a set of skills that are applicable to almost any decision, large or small, professional or personal.

WHY THIS BOOK NOW?

It's a wild time. Every day, each of us faces more choices than our grandparents confronted in a lifetime: what to say, wear, eat, think, read, watch; what to accomplish; who to be. And not only can we make any of a dozen or a hundred choices at a given moment, but we also have to deal with all the information available to us *about* those choices and then figure out what's relevant in making our decision.

And it keeps accelerating. In 2000, a research group at the University of California, Berkeley, estimated the amount of new information produced that year at 250 megabytes for every man, woman, and child on the planet. A megabyte is roughly the amount of data in a five-hundred-page book. Think about that: 6 billion people times 250 thick books' worth of *new* information, each and every year.

How on earth can we usefully sort through this onslaught of information and possibility to create the life, the career, the business we want for ourselves?

Helping people answer that question is the core of my work: it's at the heart of the consulting and coaching practice I've built with my colleagues over the past twenty years. When people ask what my company does, I say we help organizations and individuals "clarify and move toward their hoped-for future." That's another way of saying we support our clients in deciding what's most important to them, of all the possibilities available, and then making the choices that will keep them moving in that direction. Whether we're meeting one-on-one with the executives we coach or working with the senior teams of our client companies, we offer them skills and guidelines for defining and then crafting the career or the organization they envision. I intend, in writing this book, to share those approaches with you, to give you a way to make sense of what's around you—so that, even though we may never meet face-to-face, you'll be better able to "choose well": to clarify and move toward your own hoped-for future. In fact, I'd like to propose to you a definition for being strategic, based on that capability:

 Being strategic means consistently making those core directional choices that will best move you toward your hoped-for future.

This is, I think, a deceptively simple sentence. It implies that you know where you're starting from, you're clear on where you want to go, and you have the means and the will to make consistently good and powerful choices about how to get there. You can use this capability that I call being strategic to guide you through this wild time of ours.

Most important, especially for our purposes here, I think that being strategic is primarily a learnable skill. When I share this idea with others, they're generally surprised: I've noticed that when people say of someone "he [or she] isn't

5

very strategic," they use the same tone as if they were saying the person can't sing or has poor eyesight—as if the lack of strategic thinking is something built-in, irrevocable. Certainly some people have more natural talent in this area than do others, but I've come to believe (and have had my belief confirmed over and over) that almost anyone can improve his or her ability to think and act strategically—and reap the professional and personal rewards that follow.

A WORD ABOUT PURPOSE

Someone for whom I have a lot of respect asked me, on reading the initial manuscript for this book, how my definition of being strategic relates to "purpose" or "mission." I'll talk about this more specifically later in the book, when I discuss helping a group define their mission as the foundation for being strategic about the future of their organization, but I also want to address it in a general way here, as we're getting started. The beauty of being strategic as I've defined it, of thinking and acting in this way, is that it's almost universally useful. Whether your "hoped-for future" is something as straightforward and practical as "I want to be the head of my department" or as deeply purpose driven as "I want to find the work that's most satisfying to me and most beneficial to the world," you will be much more likely to achieve it if you get very clear about what it is you want and then consistently make the core directional choices. . . .

And at this point, I also want to reemphasize that this capability isn't something just for leaders, business development execs, or consultants; I've known assistants and sales clerks, homemakers and carpenters, who demonstrate this capacity. Having this capacity makes them more effective at what they do. An example: think about being served by a waitress who's just trying to get through her shift and who sees you—if she thinks about it at all—as an impediment to her ability to take a cigarette break. Now think about the experience of being served by a waitress who's putting herself through school and knows that the better the job she does serving you, the bigger the tip she's going to get and the more likely she is to be able to pay for school and graduate next spring. One is just going through the motions, and one is consistently making those core directional choices. . . . You get the idea. The essence of what we'll be talking about here is strategy as a way of seeing and living your life, a set of mental models and a way of acting on them that allows you to *create the kind of life you want.*

BEING STRATEGIC WITH A GROUP

But what about the "team" aspect of being strategic? You can find shelves full of books that tell you how important it is to "have a strategy" for your business. And I do agree that's important—I just think the way most businesses go about doing strategic planning isn't as effective as it could be. Quite often businesses "hire a strategy person" or create a "strategic planning function," as though strategy is something esoteric and apart from daily work life, an arcane lore that only certain people can understand and master. And all too often—to my earlier point about a lack of common definition—"strategy" is used to mean simply financial business modeling (financial modeling is important, but it can become an unfortunate substitute for thinking holistically about the business you want to create). I believe that approaching business strategically can be much more "normal" than all this—and that those most closely involved, day to day, in a business's success can and should craft the strategic direction for that business.

Strategy that's developed in this way is integral as opposed to extrinsic: people understand it and are committed to it; they know why it's important and what it will take to make it happen. It becomes an agreed-upon map for action that everyone shares and to which everyone is able to refer in deciding how to operate day to day.

I've also been witness to the myriad problems that can arise when people haven't developed this capability to be strategic. In working with a wide variety of people in many different kinds of organizations—and also as a citizen, friend, and parent—I've seen careers stall out, people lose sight of their true intentions and drift into lives that don't satisfy them, teams devolve into useless wrangling, and companies wander down unprofitable and ill-considered paths, all for the lack of good, clear, comprehensive strategic thinking and action.

HOW WE'LL DO THIS

Because I want you to be able to think and behave differently by the time you've finished this book, I'll approach this topic in the same way I approach coaching executives or working with senior teams: it will be a blend of theory and practice, complete with definitions and explanations, calls for self-reflection, and suggestions for things to try and things to think about. Of course, since we're not actually sitting together in the same room, we'll have to be a little creative in our "conversation." For that reason, I've tried to make this book flexible enough to accommodate your preferred approach to learning. You may be the sort of person who likes to read straight through a whole book and then do the activities later, or it may appeal to you more to read in small chunks, with time for thought and trying it out in between, or you might want to read and do the activities in exactly the way they're offered. Any way that works for you is fine with me: my only wish is that, by the end of our time together, you feel that you know what it means to be strategic, why it's important to you to have this capability, and how to do it.

So, let's explore this together. In the first part of the book, I'll expand on the simple definition I've offered here and teach you a practical approach for being strategic—including both skills and mind-set—that you can use every day, in every aspect of your life. Then, in the second part of the book, I'll teach you how to apply your strategic skills and mind-set in working with groups, so that you can help any collection of people—from your team at work to the board of your favorite charity or your kids' school's fund-raising committee—to clarify and move toward their hoped-for future. Just to give you a sense of the path before us, and what you'll read and do along the way, here's a summary of the ideas and skills you'll find in each chapter:

1. THE CASTLE ON THE HILL

Here comes the metaphor: throughout the book I'll use the idea of building a castle on a hill as a metaphor for the process of thinking strategically. In this first chapter I'll introduce a historical example of castle building that we'll keep coming back to throughout the book. In addition, I'll offer an example of a company my colleagues and I helped to reinvent their future by using this approach.

Part I: Being Strategic Every Day

2. DEFINING THE CHALLENGE: HOW CAN WE ... ?

Whether you're trying to achieve something purely practical (building an actual castle) or to understand and fulfill your overall purpose in life, getting clear about your core challenge is an essential foundation for being strategic. In this chapter, I'll share with you an approach for focusing your thinking, so that you can clearly define the areas about which you want to think strategically. I'll provide business and personal examples of those aha moments when a challenge crystallized, and then I'll help you learn to create those ahas for yourself: to define the essence of the challenge facing you.

3. WHAT IS: PULLING BACK THE CAMERA

If you were really going to build a castle on a hill, it would be essential to make sure you had a clear understanding of your current situation before beginning. You'd ask questions like: "How many people are there to help build?" "What skills do they have?" "Is there stone around we can use, or will we have to import it?" You'd also look to the past, to see what's been tried before, and whether it worked: Has anyone built a castle on this hill in times past? If so, what happened to it? This chapter will explore the first step in being strategic: getting clear about "what is," that is, the most important parts of the current situation, including how the current situation has evolved from the past.

4. WHAT'S THE HOPE: REASONABLE ASPIRATION

Imagine a group of castle builders standing in the valley, all in agreement about their current situation. Then imagine they just start racing up the hill to begin building, without agreeing on their vision for the castle. Some people stop halfway up the slope and begin building grass huts; some people get all the way to the top and start laying out the foundations for a marble palace; yet a third contingent starts arguing with everyone—they think the whole group should be putting up geodesic domes! This chapter explores the importance of clarifying the future you intend before beginning to move toward it. I'll teach you an approach for clearly envisioning your hoped-for future—in any area of your life or business.

5. WHAT'S IN THE WAY: FACING THE FACTS

Once you know where you're starting from and where you want to go, the next step is to look very clearly at the impediments that lie between you and the achievement of your goal. In our "castle on the hill" metaphor, you're still standing in the valley. You're clear about the resources available to you. You're all in agreement about the kind of castle you want. Now it's time to get clear about the obstacles you're going to have to overcome in order to create your castle. Are there sheer rock faces between you and the top of the hill? Are there trolls lurking under the bridge? You'd better find out before you begin. In this chapter, I'll talk about this part of the process of being strategic and explore why people so often avoid it. Then I'll share ways to stay open to information about potential difficulties even when it feels uncomfortable or disheartening, so you can assess the obstacles in your path with accuracy and hopefulness.

6. WHAT'S THE PATH: ROADWAY FIRST, THEN ASPHALT

OK. You're standing in the valley, you've got your blueprints for the castle, and you know where the trolls and sinkholes are on the way to the top. So, do you just pick up your tools and start walking uphill? No. First, you need to make foundational decisions about how you're going to approach this massive undertaking. This step of the process is central to being strategic—and is the point where many people, even if they've made it this far, are most likely to run off the rails and just start "doing stuff." I'll show you how this is the critical juncture in any endeavor—the point where people tend to devolve into tactics and where staying focused on the big picture is most essential to overall success.

7. THE ART OF CRAFTING STRATEGY

This chapter is the heart of the book. Selecting effective strategies to achieve your vision allows you to consistently make those choices that will best help you achieve the future you've envisioned. It gives you a framework for making best use of resources, deciding which actions to take, and staying focused on the things that are most important to you. Ironically, this part of being strategic is generally thought of as the least practical and most esoteric. (Highly paid consultants speaking strange languages! Big binders full of unintelligible jargon! No connection to day-to-day reality!) I'll demystify strategy for you by teaching you, practically and simply, how to select strategies that will move you toward your hoped-for future and that will provide the best basis for choosing tactics.

8. TACTICS THAT WORK

Good tactical planning is the final step in strategic thinking. Whether you're building a castle, a career, or a department, this is the point where you decide the specific "who, what, and when" that will take you from where you are now to where you want to go. I'll show you how to use your strategies as a basis for determining these tactics: good strategies serve as a "screening device" to help you choose the things you *most need* to do from the thousands of things you *could* do to move toward your vision. In this chapter, I'll discuss the main ways in which people get derailed during tactical planning, and then give you a chance to complete this part of the process.

9. BUILDING ON SUCCESS

Renovating your castle ought to be easier and faster than building it initially, if you have a way to assess what worked and what didn't the first time around and to incorporate that understanding into your process. This chapter will focus on reviewing the work you've done to implement your strategic plan and then "repositioning" for even better results going forward. First I'll talk about how to set up a simple system to hold yourself accountable for implementing your strategy; then I'll teach you an approach for learning from what's happened, without getting distracted by blame or finger-pointing (even at yourself).

10. THE CASTLE OF YOU

Now that you understand "strategy" and "being strategic" and you have the practical tools at your command, I'll encourage you to think through one very important way you might use your new skills. Throughout the book, I'll discuss and demonstrate the different steps of the model in a wide variety of situations: in this chapter, I'll reflect on the lives of real people who have achieved their dreams—whatever those dreams might be—by using the principles of strategic thought and action we've explored here. Then, with these folks as clarifying and inspiring models, you'll have the chance to use your newly honed skills to make an overall plan for the career and life *you* want. At the end of this last chapter in part 1, you'll create self-talk to help you stay focused and positive as you move toward your hoped-for future.

Part II: Being Strategic with a Group

11. INVITING OTHERS INTO THE PROCESS

In this chapter, I'll provide an overview of the similarities and differences between applying your "being strategic" skills and mind-set personally and applying them as a member of a group. When working with a group or team, you need to invite them into the process. I'll offer you a way of doing this that's most likely to generate curiosity, enthusiasm, and—ultimately—willing participation, so they can also benefit from this approach. We'll continue with our castle-building example, this time focusing on what it took to get others involved in and committed to the process.

12. CRAFTING A STRATEGIC VISION

Over the past twenty years, I've supported dozens of teams and companies in being strategic. I've found out a lot about how to apply this approach in a group setting and have learned even more from my colleagues at Proteus International as they work with their clients on being strategic. In this chapter I'll share with you the essence of what we've learned: practical techniques and approaches for "translating" each of the steps of being strategic into a group setting.

13. THE ART OF FACILITATION

Being able to help a group think and act strategically requires not only being able to think and act that way yourself (and knowing how to modify the process for a group) but also having some skills for supporting the group to move through the process well. In this chapter, I'll offer you core skills for group facilitation. A bonus: these skills are—as Marty Seldman, a former business partner, used to say—"core, multi-use skills." You can use the facilitation skills you'll learn in this chapter to manage any kind of meeting or group process.

14. STRATEGY AS A WAY OF LIFE

In this chapter, I'll focus on how to help groups hold themselves accountable to the strategic vision they've created. I'll also discuss how to facilitate a "repositioning" meeting after four to six months and a full "vision reboot" after twelve to eighteen months, to help the group reflect on and learn from what they've done and to revise their original plan as needed to keep moving toward their hoped-for future. In other words, you'll learn how to keep the process going past the initial vision and strategy session—so that your group actually uses the "strategic map" they've created as a guidance system for their own success.

15. CASTLE BUILDING FOR FUN AND PROFIT

I'd be really sad if you read this book, found it valuable, and then didn't use what you learned! So, this final chapter of the book gives you a chance to decide how to keep deepening your understanding and application of this approach. I'll talk about how people get in the way of their own learning—and how to keep that from happening. You'll make a few commitments to yourself, things you intend to do in order to support yourself in becoming ever more strategic in your thinking and your approach. Finally, I'll encourage you to create a simple memory aid to remind yourself why this is something you want to do—and to reaffirm your ability to do it.

That's it. In the first chapter I'll offer a more in-depth explanation of the basic model for being strategic, and then we'll spend the rest of our time together digging into the model, taking it apart, and putting it back together. I'll give you chances to practice each part of it. By the time you turn the final page, I want you to feel that you can use this model to think more clearly and act more successfully: by yourself and with others, as a boss and as a member of a team, with your spouse or children—and in challenges as personal as planning for the perfect job or as large-scale and impactful as determining the future of your company.

I truly hope you'll find this book engaging, enjoyable, and useful to you in every part of your life. If you'd like to let me know what you thought about it or find out more about my company and the work we do, I'd love to hear from you; please feel free to e-mail me at connect@proteus-international.com.

Bon voyage!

—ERIKA ANDERSEN
West Park, NY
July 18, 2008

ONE

The Castle on the Hill

I'm fascinated by castles. It's one of the many reasons I love Wales, a quirky, ancient little country with more castles per square mile than any other country in Europe. I'm fascinated by them at least partly because they provide such a grand metaphor for the idea of thinking strategically. There's a castle of which I'm especially fond: it sits up on a hill, tucked away in the far northwest corner of Wales, with the little village of Criccieth spread out around it. There's not much left of the castle now—parts of two gatehouse towers and some low stone walls—but you can squint your eyes and see what it would have looked like eight hundred years ago, high on its promontory overlooking both Cardigan Bay and the surrounding countryside. (For more about Criccieth and its castle, go to www.beingstrategic.com.)

Imagine what must have been required to create such an edifice, all those hundreds of years ago. Not just the building of it—the months or years of grueling labor in all kinds of weather; people and animals, tools and stone—but more than that. Thinking through the idea and then pulling together the diverse resources and support needed to make it a reality—all without benefit of modern machines, modern technology, or modern communication.

And I realize it could only have arisen from a very clear intention, sustained over time: *consistently making those core directional choices that will best move you toward your hoped-for future*. In short, successfully building a castle, especially on a cliff over the sea in the wild northwest of Wales in 1230, called for *someone* to be very strategic.

That someone was a guy named Llewellyn Fawr (pronounced "Thloo-ell in Vahr"), Prince of North Wales at the time. "Fawr" means roughly "the Great" in Welsh, so you can see what folks thought of him (and his castles) even then. Let's follow him around for a little while in our imagination, just to get a feel for him being strategic.

Llewellyn stands on the beach, looking out at the Irish raiders in their boats. He and his men have just beaten them back into the sea, and he's wondering yet again how he can keep his lands intact and thriving, how he can fend off not only the Irish but also the Normans, the Danes, and whoever else wants a piece of his domain. He thinks to himself: How can we best protect and defend ourselves from our enemies?

He thinks about all his resources and difficulties. On the one hand, the Welsh are brave and tough, good fighters and loyal to their prince. They know the land and how to best live on it and work it. Their farms and hunters provide enough to feed and clothe them, and they're not dependent on outsiders for necessities. On the other hand, like any land-based people, they're at the mercy of the weather, and they don't have a ready source for new or better weaponry. They have a number of enemies, but they're somewhat protected on the east by the high, rugged mountains. Having the sea on their other borders means enemies are easy to spot long before they arrive. He knows the Irish are spread very thin and are trying to do too much right now. However, he also knows the Normans, in the other direction, aren't spread thin—and their endless urge for conquest is deeply worrying.

He also thinks about history. He knows his father's and grandfathers' successes, and he knows their mistakes. For instance, he's learned from the past that fortifications built from wood are neither very secure nor very permanent, and that building in high places works well, from both a defensive and an offensive standpoint. He knows what his people are passionate about and what isn't important to them. They care about the land and their families and being independent—and they have traditionally cared less about abstract ideals of nation and statecraft.

With this clear sense of himself and his people—of where they've come from, what they have going for them, and what they're up against—Llewellyn starts to look toward the future. He calls together his nobles, and he shares with them his reflections on their common history and their current situation. Then he says to them—in thirteenth-century Welsh, of course— "So, my friends, given all this, how can we best protect and defend ourselves and our people from our enemies?"

After much discussion (and many cups of mead), the group comes to the conclusion that the core of that safe and strong

*future would be a well-built, fully defensible, and strongly forti-
fied castle on the hill before them, providing excellent oversight of
the sea to the south and west and the land to the north and east.
They've got a pretty clear overall agreement on how it will work,
what it will look like, and what it will do to protect them.*

*Having agreed to that, they bid each other good night and
promise to start deciding how to make it a reality in the morn-
ing (when the mead wears off). . . .*

We'll come back to our medieval Welsh nobles in a few
minutes, but for now, here we are, back in the twenty-first
century. And I'll bet you're wondering why I've led you down
this particular path. Let me explain myself.

In the introduction (if you haven't yet read it, you may
want to go back and do so, or you'll keep wondering what I'm
talking about), I told you that from my point of view, being
strategic is a learnable skill, like playing chess or doing car-
pentry. And like both of those skills, being strategic involves
learning to think in specific, patterned ways and then acting
based on that thinking.

I'm using Llewellyn, his men (sorry it's all men—remember,
this is the thirteenth century), and his castle to talk about this
way of thinking and acting because it's just such a wonderful
example—and also because it allows me to then use the metaphor of "the castle on the hill" throughout the book! So, let's
go back to Llewellyn and his entourage and see what they do
next:

*The Welshmen meet again around the council table bright
and early the next day, ready to figure out how to achieve that*

safe and strong future they've envisioned for themselves, that castle on the hill.

First, though, Llewellyn encourages them to think about what they're going to have to overcome in order to do this. One guy, Gryffudd (pronounced "Griffith"), notes that they haven't built a castle like this before; they've only made wooden hill forts. Some others point out that the hill is really steep and while that's great in terms of defense from enemies, it's going to make it a real pain getting men and supplies up there to build the thing. Finally, Dafydd (pronounced "Dah-vith") and Owain (pronounced "Oh-wayn"), the captains of the guard, point out that there's no guarantee they won't be attacked while they're building, and they'd be more vulnerable than usual, with all their able-bodied men engaged in the construction. Llewellyn agrees with everything and throws in a few more problems: the time and energy required to transport the stone and the fact that anybody who's building the castle won't be able to tend his fields.

After that, there's a lot of talking—the Welsh are enthusiastic and skillful talkers and arguers—but by the time the sun is overhead, they've agreed on the most important efforts they need to make, given where they're starting from, where they're trying to go, and the obstacles that exist. Llewellyn summarizes, "All right, my nobles, here's what we've decided: First, we need to design the castle—a castle that will protect us and that we can build with the skills and materials we have access to. Second, we need to decide how we'll build it—the whole process from start to finish. Third, we need to figure out how to defend and provision ourselves while it's being built. Is that about it?"

All the men nod their assent. "Good," Llewellyn continues.

"Gryffudd, you're in charge of deciding the design of the thing. Ifor [pronounced 'Ih-vor'], you're in charge of figuring out how to build it. Dafydd, you and Owain create the backup defense and provisioning plan. Be back here in two weeks to recommend what, who, and when."

As the meeting breaks up, Gryffudd immediately turns to his cousin Hwyl (pronounced "Hoo-il"), who has been spying on the Norman fortifications in Shrewsbury, to ask him to help create an approach for designing the castle, incorporating the techniques the Normans use so well. Ifor leaves to find Teilo (pronounced "Day-lo"), who is great at organizing men and supplies. Dafydd sits down with Owain and the biggest landholders to think about a secondary defense and provisioning plan.

They're on their way to their castle on the hill.

Now, of course, I'm mostly making this up out of whole cloth. But I can only imagine it took place *something* like this, because there it is, almost eight hundred years later, Criccieth Castle, a monument to their clear intention and well-planned execution. So let's pretend that it all happened just like this, an amazingly clear example of the model I'm about to share with you:

--- **BEING STRATEGIC** ---

Define the Challenge, then

Clarify *What Is*

Envision *What's the Hope*

Face *What's in the Way*

Determine *What's the Path*

DEFINE THE CHALLENGE: In my definition of being strategic, you'll notice that the last four words are "toward your hoped-for future." This implies, of course, that you've figured out what aspect of your future you're looking toward! Defining the challenge allows you to get clear about this. Generally, the most useful way to define your challenge is to find a "How can I . . . ?" or "How can we . . . ?" question that best summarizes the problem you're trying to solve or the goal you're trying to reach. For our Welsh prince, Llewellyn, the question was, "How can we best protect and defend ourselves from our enemies?"

1. CLARIFY *WHAT IS:* In this step of the model, you draw upon both history and your current reality to get a clear sense of where you're starting relative to your challenge. In our earlier example, Llewellyn did a kind of informal "SWOT" (Strengths, Weaknesses, Opportunities, and Threats) analysis. He focused internally on what he and his people had going for them and what they lacked—their strengths and weaknesses—but he also focused on factors external to him, ways in which he and his people were threatened by outside forces (the urge toward conquest of the Normans) and ways in which outside forces might provide opportunities for his success (the Irish being spread too thin). He also drew on his knowledge of history, reflecting on the effective and not-so-effective ways in which his forefathers had tried to defend their land.

2. ENVISION *WHAT'S THE HOPE:* This step is where you answer the core of the initial "How can we . . . ?" question. You envision a future that would address the challenge as you've defined it, given your current reality. Llewellyn's group decided that building a castle on the hill would address their challenge best. They agreed how it would work and look and what it would provide for them in terms of defense and safety. In other words, they envisioned their castle on the hill clearly enough so that they could all see it together and feel confident that if they created it according to their vision, it would address their challenge.

3. FACE *WHAT'S IN THE WAY*: At this point in the process of being strategic, you step back and look at the whole picture you've created so far. You know where you're starting from and where you want to go, so now you can look at what's in the way: the obstacles in between your "what is" and the future you envision. Llewellyn and his men thought through the key difficulties they would need to address in order to build their castle: a lack of previous experience, the inaccessibility of the site, their vulnerability during the construction period, the difficulty of transporting the stone, and the fact that anybody who's building the castle won't be able to tend his fields. It's essential to know what might get in the way of moving from your current reality to your hoped-for future. Then you can factor the need to get over, around, or through those obstacles into your plan.

4. DETERMINE *WHAT'S THE PATH*: In this last part of the process of being strategic, you decide first on your strategies—those core directional choices or efforts you'll need to make in order to achieve your hoped-for future. Once you've selected those strategies, you'll craft the specific tactics that will best implement them. Here's how Llewellyn described the core directional efforts for building his castle: "First, we need to *design the castle*—a castle that will protect us and that we can build with the skills and materials we have access to. Second, we need to *decide how we'll build it*—the whole process from start to finish. Third, we need to *figure out how to defend and provision ourselves while it's being built.*" Once he and his men agreed on these three strategies, he sent out some of his guys to come up with tactical plans—to determine the who, what, and when required to implement each of the three strategies.

Figure 1 shows how my colleagues and I visualize this process; we find it often helps people to think of it as a literal journey toward a goal.

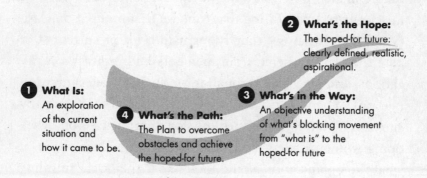

2 What's the Hope:
The hoped-for future: clearly defined, realistic, aspirational.

1 What Is:
An exploration of the current situation and how it came to be.

4 What's the Path:
The Plan to overcome obstacles and achieve the hoped-for future.

3 What's in the Way:
An objective understanding of what's blocking movement from "what is" to the hoped-for future

Figure 1

EIGHT HUNDRED YEARS LATER

Lest you think this process applies only to conveniently simple medieval situations, let me offer a present-day business example to demonstrate the usefulness of this way of thinking and acting.

Some years ago, a non-profit organization came to us and asked if we could help them reinvent themselves. They wanted to regain their position as the premier women's group in their industry: membership growth had stalled and the programs they offered their members were unfocused and uneven in execution. They weren't sure who they wanted to be or where they wanted to go. They had hired a new, high-profile CEO and tasked her with creating a new strategic plan for the organization.

First, we helped them to define their challenge. They realized the heart of it was, "How can we revitalize our organization to be the best resource available for the women in our industry?" They brought together a strategic planning committee made up of board members and senior staff, and we met for two days. During that time we first focused on clarifying their "what is" (they brought in a lot of current state data they had gathered from members and industry organizations, and we sorted through it for the most relevant information). Then they envisioned their hoped-for future by agreeing on a new, simplified mission that focused on developing women leaders, and then agreeing on their vision of what the organization would look like if they were fulfilling that mission. Once they had done that, they looked at the obstacles to achieving the vision, both inside and outside the organization; they were especially honest about the fact that their current not-so-great reputation was a challenge to be overcome.

At that point, everyone in the group felt they understood where they were starting from (point A), where they wanted to go (point B), and what was in the way. I then helped them to define their path from point A to point B: choosing those core directional efforts that would best move them from their current state toward their envisioned future. At the end of two days and a lot of great, in-depth conversation, they had a "map"—a handful of strategies and the tactics to implement them—they felt would allow them to achieve their vision.

The great thing was, they didn't stop there. They incorporated this more strategic approach into their ongoing thought and action. They met regularly to continue working on their strategies, and they made a habit of coming together yearly to review their mission and vision and revise their strategies and tactics to reflect the work they had done and keep them moving toward their vision.

Now, seven years later, the organization has doubled its membership and refined its programmatic offer to focus on leadership development for women. They've also partnered with another women's organization to develop a highly regarded initiative that works with industry organizations to assess their progress on key issues affecting women. They've achieved much of what they set out to do in that initial session, so this summer they met again to "re-vision"—to decide the next chapter in the future they want to create for themselves.

ON TO YOUR DESIRED OUTCOMES

Enough of introduction and overview; it's time for the practical skills of being strategic. In the first half of the book, beginning with the next chapter, we'll focus on the individual level. You'll learn how to approach any situation in your life more strategically, in order to clarify and create the future you want.

In the second half of the book, we'll explore how you can adapt this process to help a group be more strategic in their approach. You'll learn how to share and apply the habits of thought and action from the first half of the book, using techniques and skills my colleagues and I have used over the years in helping our client companies to be more strategic.

Throughout, Llewellyn, his people, and his castle will be our companions. Let's get started!

In Real Life:

Start to look for this pattern—*"what is," "what's the hope," "what's in the way," "what's the path"*—in successful lives and enterprises. When you read or hear about someone making a big change in his or her life or the world, or about an organization that's achieving its goals, see if you can recognize these four steps of being strategic embedded in the story. Once you can see the basic shape of this process in these endeavors, it will begin to make sense as a practical approach.

PART ONE

BEING STRATEGIC EVERY DAY

TWO

Defining the Challenge: How Can We . . . ?

Llewellyn's horse moves restlessly beneath him as he sits gazing down to the beach below. The women and children gathering the Irish fleet's spent arrows on the shingle move quickly; they've done this too many times before.

Owain and Dafydd, Llewellyn's captains, sit astride their own horses to either side of him. "We should go after the bloody Irish," Owain says. "I'm tired of them swooping in on us like this. We lost five good men this time—not to mention the farmstead they burned before we drove them off."

Dafydd shakes his head. "They've got too many ships. They'd slaughter us." He turns to Llewellyn. "My lord, we should call up the men from around Conwy, so that next time the Irish come—"

"Why should they come to our aid when they—," Owain begins, irritated.

Llewellyn puts up a hand. "I know we're all angry, but we

can't just jump at solutions like this. We'll spend all our time and men trying one thing after another." He looks at both of them. "And it's not just the Irish; you know that. It's whoever decides to attack us—the Normans, the Danes. We've got to find a solid way to protect ourselves."

Dafydd frowns. "How can we do that?"

Llewellyn looks at him, eyes narrowed in thought. "That's the question, isn't it? How can we best protect and defend ourselves from our enemies?"

Our man Llewellyn has just gone directly to the heart of it: what you've just witnessed is the first step toward being strategic. He's just "defined the challenge" instead of getting into an argument, which is what most often happens when people don't define the challenge.

PROBLEM FIRST, SOLUTION SECOND

In my experience, people often propose solutions to problems before they're clear on what the problem is. Individuals do it; teams do it; companies do it. For instance, how often have you sat in a meeting and listened while people argued the merits of various courses of action? ("We should do this." "No, it will work far better if we do this.") All too often, the reason people feel so strongly about very different solutions is that they have very different implicit assumptions about the problem.

Let's use Owain and Dafydd as an example. What if Llewellyn hadn't turned their attention to the real problem? The preceding conversation would have taken a very different path: Owain would have focused on convincing Dafydd that a sea battle with the Irish was the way to go, and Dafydd would have focused on convincing Owain that reinforcements from Conwy were their best shot. As you can imagine, the discussion would have devolved pretty quickly into a frustrating argument, with each of them proposing solutions that made no sense to the other. And they would have been no closer to understanding—and therefore being able to solve—their real problem.

THE ACTUAL CHALLENGE

Let me remind you again (soon it will be burned into your memory, for better or for worse) of my proposed definition for being strategic: *consistently making those core directional choices that will best move you toward your hoped-for future.*

Discovering the real problem—the core challenge in a given situation—is the necessary preamble to this definition. Until you have a clear sense of the problem to be solved, it's impossible to envision what "solved" would look like—that is, the future you want to create. Without being able to see that, how can you decide the core directional choices you'll need to make to get there?

So, how do you get to the real challenge? I'll give you a hint: ask questions. As you've noticed, what generally prevents us from discovering the real problem is coming up with answers too quickly. The approach I'd like to offer you for defining the real challenge involves shifting that dynamic by asking yourself some very specific questions:

———————— **DEFINING THE CHALLENGE** ————————

Ask: What isn't working?

Ask: How can we (or I) . . . ?

Ask: Would this feel like success?

ASK: WHAT ISN'T WORKING?: People generally don't like to focus on what's not working. I believe this is the main reason we tend to move too quickly to solutions. We don't want to think about what isn't working; we want to fix it. It's fascinating to me how we slip right past the challenge. Just last week, I was working with someone to define her challenge and I asked her what wasn't working for her. And she said, "I need to—"

I gently interrupted her and noted that the phrase "I need to . . ." is invariably the beginning of a solution.

She looked confused and responded, "Yes, I'm telling you what I need to do to fix what isn't working."

"You're not quite ready to think usefully about how to fix it," I replied. "You don't yet know what it is." I could see the light go on for her at that point, and then she was able to describe fairly thoroughly what wasn't working for her in the situation we were discussing.

ASK: HOW CAN WE [OR I] . . . ?: Once you've looked, clear-eyed and unflinching, at what's not working, it's fairly easy to frame the challenge. The person I mentioned earlier was focusing on the current direction of her life, both professional and personal. And after she thought and talked through the "what's not working," her "How can I . . . ?" statement emerged almost automatically. It was: "How can I create a life that's balanced and joyful, doing work I love?" It works equally well in business: a few months ago, I worked with the marketing department of a media company and their "How can we . . . ?" was "How can we create a department that consistently thinks in fresh ways about our brand?"

ASK: WOULD THIS FEEL LIKE SUCCESS?: This is your "checking" question. It's a way to make sure you're on the right track before you begin moving toward addressing your challenge. Here's how this works. With my recent client, I asked, "So, if you create a life that's balanced and joyful, doing work you love, would that feel like success to you?"

She thought for a minute, and nodded. "Yes," she said, "that's pretty much it. There are other little minor things—but yes, if I did that, it would mean what isn't working now would be working."

If accomplishing the goal stated in your "How can we [I] . . . ?" question wouldn't feel like success, then you need to go back to the drawing board. When I asked the marketing group the same question: "So, if you create a department that consistently thinks in fresh ways about your brand, would that feel like success?" they actually said no. They realized that was only half their challenge; they also needed their fresh thinking to be meaningful to their consumers. So they changed their "How can we . . . ?" question to "How can we create a department that consistently thinks about our brand in fresh ways that create an emotional connection with the consumer?"

LEARNING TO DO THIS

One of the great things about learning to think in this way is that it pretty quickly becomes second nature. It's kind of like driving a stick-shift car or skiing. If you know how to do either of those things, I'm sure you remember how incredibly clunky it felt the first time you tried it, like you'd never be able to do it with any facility or ease. Throughout our journey together in this book, I'll be teaching you skills—new ways to think and behave—and in order to do that, I'm going to have to take them apart and give you a chance to try out the parts, and then put them together, just like learning to ski or drive or build a bookcase. It will probably feel somewhat awkward and unnatural the first couple of times, but then it will start to come together. And by the end of the book, I feel confident you'll be well on your way to being comfortably and consistently strategic in your thinking and actions.

Try It Out

I'm going to walk you through the process of defining a challenge for yourself, using the three questions in this chapter. I suggest you choose a real problem, either personal or professional, that you're facing right now. That way, at the end of the practice you'll have an outcome that's meaningful for you and this won't be just an exercise.

✓ First, select a situation or an area of your life to explore and jot down a few words to describe it. You're doing this simply to turn your attention toward this area as you apply the three questions. For instance, you might simply write down "my job," or "marriage," or even "my future."

_____

_____

_____

_____

_____

_____

_____

✓ **ASK: WHAT ISN'T WORKING?:** Use the space below to jot down whatever comes to mind in answer to this question. Resist any temptation to begin solving the problem (beware, especially, of sentences that begin "I need to" or "I should").

_____

_____

_____

_____

_____

_____

✓ **ASK: HOW CAN I . . . ?:** Now formulate your "How can I . . ." question, looking for a sentence that addresses the key elements of what's not working. I've left an open space, so you can try various sentences, add things, cross things out. When you've decided how you want to frame the question, complete your sentence in the box.

How can I [we]

✓ **ASK: WOULD THIS FEEL LIKE SUCCESS?:** Reread your sentence in the box, asking, "If I achieved this, would it feel like success?" If your answer is "yes," congratulations! If your answer is "no" or "not quite," think about how you need to change the question in order to more fully address what's not working. If you need to revise your "How can I . . ." question, you can write the final version in the following box.

How can I [we]

THE POWER OF "HOW CAN I [WE] . . . ?"

Once you get in the habit of asking this question, you'll find that it's a powerful tool for clarity. Often when I'm in the midst of a problem and I'm either stuck in "what's not working" (that process where you go over and over in your mind the difficulties at hand, feeling caught in an endless loop) or stuck in a wrangle with someone about how to solve it, if I stop, pull back, and make the effort to formulate the "How can I . . . ?" or "How can we . . . ?" question, it can be like a sword cutting through confusion and disagreement.

By way of illustration, here's an example of two colleagues trying to solve a problem at work:

Jenna comes into Tom's office in a rush, her arms full of folders. "You're not gonna believe this," she says, dropping them on his desk and sinking into the nearest chair. "It turns out that when Sylvia left the company two weeks ago, she didn't complete any of the open orders on her list and she didn't tell anybody she hadn't finished them!"

Tom rolls his eyes and shakes his head. "Unbelievable. So, now what? We're supposed to somehow magically know what to do with all of them?" He riffles through the pile of folders. "There's got to be twenty of them here."

"I know," Jenna replies, shaking her head. "And remember, they're all at least two weeks old."

"Have you told the boss?" Tom asks.

"He's in Tampa for a conference," Jenna says. "And, I don't know, do we really want to tell him? Aren't we supposed to be taking care of order processing as a team? I don't

think anything here is out of spec. They're just not finished."

"Yeah, yeah. You're right. OK, well, I'm way too busy right now. The Gainesville sales team has been going nuts, and I've got a zillion orders open."

"Come on, Tom—that's not fair! I helped you out all last week." Jenna's voice is rising. "Do you really expect Allen and me to do all of these? We're not any less busy than you are."

"You don't know what it's like with all this new Gainesville stuff, Jenna. Not only are there tons of orders, but at least half of them are for the new system, and they haven't even told me how to enter it yet." Tom pushes the folders back toward her. "You and Allen can do these; just split them up between you."

Jenna pushes them back toward Tom's side of the desk. "Tom, come on. Those Gainesville orders aren't a rush. I'll bet the Gainesville sales guys don't even have delivery dates yet. You know there's a soft hold on the final system check."

Tom frowns and takes a deep breath, ready to keep arguing.

Let's tiptoe softly away. It doesn't get any better from here. Tom and Jenna might work something out and they might not, but in either case they will have wasted a lot of time and emotional energy, and they're certainly not clear on the real challenge. They're completely focused on playing hot potato with those folders.

How about if we rewind the tape and try it again? This time, let's pretend that Tom has just read this chapter and is thinking about "How can we . . . ?" questions even as Jenna arrives.

Jenna comes into Tom's office in a rush, her arms full of folders. "You're not gonna believe this," she says, dropping them on his desk and sinking into the nearest chair. "It turns out that when Sylvia left the company two weeks ago, she didn't complete any of the open orders on her list and she didn't tell anybody she hadn't finished them!"

Tom rolls his eyes and shakes his head. "Unbelievable. So, now what? We're supposed to somehow magically know what to do with all of them?" He riffles through the pile of folders. "There's got to be twenty of them here."

"I know," Jenna replies, shaking her head. "And remember, they're all at least two weeks old."

Tom takes a deep breath. "OK. OK. Let's not panic here. So, what we're dealing with is twenty or so overdue open orders, right?"

"Yeah." Jenna nods. "Now, if you could just—"

Tom puts up his hand in a "wait a second" gesture. "Hold on; let's make sure we're clear about the problem first. Have you looked through the folders yet?"

"A little. They're mostly for existing customers. But there are a few—five maybe—for brand-new accounts. I hate that they've been just sitting there." Jenna shakes her head in frustration.

"And I'm really swamped right now. How about you and Allen?"

Jenna chews her lip. "I'm pretty busy, and so's Allen."

"OK." Tom thinks for a minute. "It seems to me the question is: How can we close these orders in a way that's best for

the customers and is fairest to the three of us, given our exist-
ing workloads?"

Jenna's nodding, starting to look relieved. "Yeah, best for
the customer, fairest to us. That's right. OK, so I guess that
means we should do the oldest ones first, and also the ones for
the brand-new customers. We don't want them to get a bad
first impression about our turnaround."

"Yeah," Tom agrees. "Let's get Allen in here, so we can
work this out together." He picks up the phone, and they're on
the way to a solution . . .

Wouldn't you rather have the second conversation? When
people take the time to define the challenge, it turns their attention in a new, far more productive direction. Instead of
focusing on trying to convince themselves or others of the
rightness of their solution or the legitimacy of their com-
plaint, they begin to focus on solving the actual problem.

In Real Life:

Think of situations you've been in over the past few weeks where you got
stuck in complaining (over-focusing on "what's not working") or in "duel-
ing solutions." See if you can come up with a "how can I [we]" question
that might have redirected your energy.

THREE

What Is: Pulling Back the Camera

Llewellyn is tired, cold, and saddlesore, but at least he's reasonably certain that his people are in good heart and will be able to repair the damage the Irish have inflicted during this latest raid. He's shared his condolences with those who've lost husbands, fathers, and sons and made sure that the family whose farm was burned has somewhere to lodge for now. Now that he's riding back to his own hall, he starts to think again about how he can best protect and defend his people and his land, and he realizes suddenly that it's just like beginning a battle. He needs to know what resources he has to use.

Owain and Dafydd are still riding to either side of him, looking even more worn-out than he feels. They've spent the whole day working to help those friends and neighbors hardest hit by the raid.

"If we're going to figure this out," Llewellyn says suddenly, "how best to protect and defend ourselves, we have to know where we're starting from."

Dafydd, roused from a half doze, looks confused. "Start-ing from?" he asks.

"Yes," Lllewellyn says. "What we have to work with. It's like we're gathering men for a battle, but bigger than that: all the things that would help or hinder us from protecting or de-fending ourselves."

"Ah," Owain says, understanding. "We're good fighters, and we're loyal. And we're self-sufficient. We grow or hunt almost all that we need. And the land helps. The mountains make it harder for the Normans to get to us."

Dafydd's still grouchy with sleep. "We don't come together very well, though," he says. "We Welsh are an independent lot. They're loyal to you, Lord," he adds, nodding to Llewellyn, "but not much beyond that."

Llewellyn looks thoughtful. "That's all true," he agrees. "Now, what about the Normans and the Irish? We need to think clearly about their strengths and weaknesses, too, if we're to know how to best protect ourselves from them. . . ."

Our prince is going about this the right way. I've said (a number of times now) that being strategic is focusing consis-tently toward your hoped-for future. Once you've defined your challenge, so you know the part of your future you're looking at, it's a natural impulse to want to start defining that "hope" immediately, responding to the challenge. What I've found over the years, though, is that it's essential to be clear about where you're starting from before you can think pro-ductively about where you want to go. For instance, Llewellyn and his guys could have had fun deciding that the best way to protect and defend themselves was to build a Great Wall of Wales, shutting out everyone else, but that wouldn't have been remotely realistic (or even desirable) given their circumstances and resources.

So, before you start thinking about the answer to your "How can we [I] . . . ?" question, I suggest you spend some time getting a clear sense of your beginning point, your current reality. I call it the "what is." You've done a little of this already in defining the challenge—you've identified what isn't working for you about your current situation. But now you need to expand your view and allow in *all* the relevant information. That will become your foundation for envisioning what your desired future will look like and then how to get from where you are now to where you want to be.

For example, when I'm working with coaching clients, they are very often focused on getting to the next level in their careers. (In other words, that's an important "how can I . . . ?" for them). But before they start thinking about what it would be like to be a Senior VP, or how to get there, I have them reflect on their current situation, looking first at what they bring to the party: that is, at their own strengths and weaknesses relevant to this challenge. For instance: Do they have the needed skills and experience? Have they developed strong relationships with those who are important to their success? Then I have them look outside themselves at relevant factors in the environment around them. Is their boss supportive of their advancement? Does their company tend to promote from within? How easy or difficult is it for people in their position to find higher-level jobs in their field?

HOW TO LOOK AND WHAT TO LOOK FOR

I've noticed, over the years, that people tend to err in one of two directions when trying to objectively assess their current situation in this way. Either they look too narrowly, over-focusing on one or two aspects of the "what is" or they focus too broadly, trying to look at every single aspect of their current reality.

On the one hand, when you look too narrowly at the "what is," you won't have all the information you need, and so will likely be less successful in addressing the challenge. For instance, if someone who wants to be promoted over-focuses on her boss's lack of support, she might overlook the critical fact that she's missing essential skills or experience for the bigger job or that someone else on the team is more qualified. (This is a classic example of what people tend to mean when they say someone is being "too tactical"—that he or she is only looking at a few aspects of the situation and not clearly seeing the bigger picture.)

On the other hand, when you look *too* broadly at the current situation, without any filtering mechanisms, you can get overwhelmed by data and become unable to make sense of your starting point. All too often, I see this happen in traditional "strategic planning" processes, where huge amounts of time and energy are spent gathering up vast quantities of information, which is then presented to a senior group with no sense of what aspects of it may be more or less relevant to the organization's core challenges (which, all too often, have also not been clearly defined). I recently worked with an organization that had been involved in a yearlong process of data gathering as the first step in a multi-phase strategic planning process. The CEO called us in because he was starting to worry—rightly—that the highly paid consultants were simply going to dump the data on him and present their own conclusions about where the organization should go, rather than summarizing the data in a way that would allow him and his team to define their *own* hoped-for future.

WHAT IF YOU DON'T LIKE THE "WHAT IS"?

There's one other factor that limits our ability to get clear about the relevant elements of our current situation—our pre-existing beliefs and preferences. In fact, the single biggest obstacle to seeing reality clearly might be our wide variety of implicit beliefs about what is and isn't important, what is and isn't possible, what is and isn't true. For example, we are often quite inaccurate in our assessment of what *we* bring to a situation. We may believe that we are more or less capable than we actually are, or we may over- or under-estimate our impact on others. Or we may neglect to include things that simply don't serve our hopes. For instance, if we would prefer to believe that we're the best candidate for a job, it's easy to ignore someone else's qualifications.

So, in order to clearly understand your starting point, you need to look at your current situation in a way that's objective and that's inclusive and yet focused. Here's an approach for doing that.

CLARIFYING "WHAT IS"

Become a "Fair Witness"

Pull back the camera

Sort for impact

BECOME A "FAIR WITNESS": I have to fess up. I stole this phrase from Robert Heinlein and I use it all the time. In his book, *Stranger in a Strange Land,* Heinlein invents a profession where people are trained to be absolutely impartial in their assessments and to speak only from their direct observation, without inference or speculation. If you point to a white house and ask one of Heinlein's Fair Witnesses what color it is, he or she will say, "It appears to be painted white on this side."

In order to be strategic, it's important to cultivate this ability. When you're clarifying the "what is" relative to a challenge you've defined, ask yourself whether you're being a Fair Witness. Are you stating things as they really are or as you'd like them to be? Are you neglecting or ignoring facts that aren't comfortable or convenient? Are you assuming some things aren't important simply because you don't want to factor them into your thinking? Include in your thinking about the "what is" all those things Heinlein's Fair Witnesses would include.

For example, let's say that the challenge you've defined is the one from the end of the last chapter, with Tom and Jenna: "How can we close these orders in a way that's best for the customers and fairest to the three of us, given our workloads?" It would be easy for Tom to overstate his workload, focusing more heavily on the Gainesville orders than was perhaps strictly accurate, in order to make a case for his not having to do as many of the open orders. But if he was committed to being a Fair Witness, as a way to properly define the "what is" he would make an effort to be as accurate as possible in reporting his current workload to his colleagues.

PULL BACK THE CAMERA: Imagine a scene in a movie. The camera is pulled in tight, and all you see is a lamp on a table. Looks pretty ordinary. The camera pans back, and you see that the lamp and the table are sitting in a completely empty room, with no other furniture, no curtains on the windows. Hmm, what's going on here? Now it's not quite ordinary. The camera pans back again, through the window and out to the street. Now you see the whole house; there's a real estate sign on the front lawn with a Sold sticker pasted across it. Suddenly, it all makes sense.

You can do the same thing in your mind as you look at a situation you're in. Let's say you're the head of sales for a company and you've asked yourself: "How can we increase sales in a sustainable way?" (It's a good "How can we ... ?" question.) You know that one salesperson is consistently missing his targets. It's easy to assume that he's not competent. But if, instead, you "pull back the camera" and look at the larger situation around that person, you might see that the new product line he's primarily responsible for selling isn't performing as promised because there's a manufacturing glitch. The high return level is affecting both his current sales numbers and his customers' willingness to reorder. Hmmm. The broader view gives a very different perspective.

SORT FOR IMPACT: If you've ever built a house of cards, you know some cards are essential to the integrity of the structure and

BEING STRATEGIC EVERY DAY

some aren't. Take a card off the top—no problem. Remove a card near the bottom—good-bye, card house. If you want to be a successful card house builder, it's important to know the difference.

Similarly, distinguishing those facts or events that most impact the current situation from those that don't is an important part of getting clear about "what is." For instance, in the previous sales example, when you pull back the camera to look at the larger situation around the salesperson, let's say you immediately learn two additional things: that he eats a sandwich for lunch every day and that he has a new boss, with whom he doesn't seem to be getting along. Which of those things do you imagine might be most impacting the current situation? Most people would immediately put aside the "sandwich" information and include the "new boss" fact in their overall "what is" picture. Sorting the information you receive for its probable impact on the challenge you've defined allows you to see the big picture without being distracted by less relevant details. (Now you can see a key reason that it's important to define the challenge first.)

Try It Out

Let's try this out, using your "How can we [I] . . . ?" question from the previous chapter.

✓ Think of your challenge. You can turn back to p. 39 to refresh your memory, or you can rewrite it below:

How can I [we]

✓ **BECOME A FAIR WITNESS:** As you begin to think about the current situation, make an agreement with yourself to be as impartial and objective—as "Fair Witness"—as you can be. As you work through the following two steps, ask yourself: What am I missing? What am I misrepresenting? (If there are parts of the current situation where you feel you can't be objective or important elements you may not even know you're missing, you can ask someone else who knows the situation well to "spot" you by filling in the blanks or pushing back on your assessment. In fact, you may want to show your results in this activity to that person, just to get his or her feedback and help you "Fair Witness.")

✓ **PULL BACK THE CAMERA:** Now, think about your challenge. Mentally "pull the camera back" so that you can see not only things directly relating to the challenge but also the broader circumstances surrounding it. First, what do you bring to this challenge: strengths and weaknesses, resources and deficiencies in resource? Then look around you: what aspects of the situation support or don't support your success in addressing this challenge? Finally: what other information do you see that's connected to your challenge? Now that you're looking at the challenge more broadly, are there critical pieces of information you're lacking in order to understand the bigger picture? (For example, executives I coach who are looking to advance their careers often realize they don't have enough information about the availability of higher-level jobs in their field.) How will you find out that information?

✓ As you look at the current situation relative to your challenge with the "camera pulled back," feel free to use the space here to jot down your thoughts (if you need more space, you might want to use another sheet of paper):

My Positives: Strengths, Skills, or Resources I Bring to This Challenge	My Negatives: Weaknesses or Lack of Skill or Resource I Bring to This Challenge
Outside Positives: Circumstances That Support Me in Addressing This Challenge	Outside Negatives: Circumstances That Might Impede Me in Addressing This Challenge

✓ **SORT FOR IMPACT:** Now, reread everything you've written here (or on your other sheet of paper) and circle the "what is" information that you believe has the most impact on your ability to address your challenge. (For instance, one executive I coached realized that his lack of an MBA wasn't really an important factor in getting promoted, given his company's culture and the field he was in; he didn't circle it.) Remember to stay in "Fair Witness" mode. Challenge yourself to be as objective as possible about the potential impact of the elements you've noted.

LETTING THE PICTURE EMERGE

Once you've worked through the preceding activity, I suggest you live with it for a couple of days and then come back and see if you want to write down anything else. You may find that your brain continues to clarify the current situation even when you're not consciously focusing on it. You may think of new information that seems relevant, or you may find yourself looking at "old" information in a new way. A few months ago, I was working with a senior legal and business affairs person in a large corporation. She wanted to figure out how to restructure and rebuild her department to make it more efficient. Once she had clarity about that "How can I . . . ?" question, I helped her think through the relevant aspects of her "what is." I thought she did an excellent and thorough job. She really pulled back the camera and was very "Fair Witness." She thought about the skills of the people in her department, the interactions between her department and their internal clients, and her own leadership skills. A few weeks later she called me and told me that she had realized there was another relevant factor: the fact that big law firms in her city offered significantly better compensation packages to starting lawyers than her company did. That element could have significant impact on her ability to address her challenge, and it didn't occur to her till she gave her brain some time to process the situation.

Once you have defined both your challenge and your current state, it's finally time to look toward your desired outcome. This is the fun part: Llewellyn envisions his castle, and you . . . ?

In Real Life:

In order to be strategic, you need to practice stretching your "pulling back the camera" muscle and your "Fair Witness" muscle. Here's an idea for doing both. Pick a situation in your life (it's easiest to start with a relatively minor one) where you feel like you've lost your objectivity. Imagine that you are a camera operator filming you in the situation. As the camera pulls back, what comes into the viewfinder? Looking at the situation as the camera operator, notice what you see others doing, what you see yourself doing, and what else comes into the picture. You may be surprised at how differently you now see the situation.

What's the Hope:
Reasonable Aspiration

"And even though King John is my father-in-law," Llewellyn *finishes, "I'm none too sure the Normans won't try to come over the mountains at us."*

The eight men sitting around the long trestle table in front of the fire nod and murmur in agreement. Llewellyn has put the challenge to them—how can we best protect and defend our-selves and our people from our enemies?—and then, before they can start arguing over the best answer, he's laid out for them what he sees as all the relevant aspects of their current situa-tion.

Huw (pronounced "Hyoo"), a landholder out toward Pwllheli, whom everyone sees as a bit of a dreamer, stares into the fire and asks, "So, what would it look like if we were well protected?"

The others shake their heads and smile, Dafydd rolling his eyes. But Llewellyn looks at Huw with interest. "What do you mean by that?"

Huw looks up from his reverie, nearly startled. "Oh, just a fancy, I suppose. I meant, if we could imagine what it would be like, being protected and defended from our enemies, maybe then we could just make that happen."

The others are still ready to mock him for his unconventional thoughts, but Llewellyn's intrigued. "No, no, stop, you lot. That makes sense to me, Huw. It's just the way I saw Gwynedd (pronounced "Gwin-eth"), as being united, and then made it come to pass." He turns to the others. "So, what would that look like?"

Owain nods, beginning to understand. "Well, we'd be making better use of the promontory over the bay, that's sure. A more defensible spot I've never seen. . . ."

And they're on their way to envisioning their hoped-for future. As Llewellyn pointed out, we tend to do this automatically when we're passionate about something. People imagine being married to the one they love; an actor envisions winning an Oscar and getting plum roles; a child imagines getting the bike he or she really wants for Christmas.

What I'm encouraging here, though, is to take that natural capacity and build on it, to learn to envision the future you want in a more fully fleshed-out way. First, you define the challenge—that is, the particular "area" of the future you want to focus on—as Llewellyn did with his "How can we best protect and defend ourselves from our enemies?" question. Then, as per the last chapter, you pull back the camera to look at all those elements of your current state that are most relevant to the challenge. Llewellyn did this by talking his council through the strengths and vulnerabilities of his people, of the land itself, and of their enemies.

Then, with the help of his friend Huw, Llewellyn made the mental shift I believe is critical to a clear vision. He began to imagine what it would look like in a future where the challenge had been addressed.

For most people, this is the fun part of being strategic: envisioning possibilities. It's also a key element of most successful lives. People who achieve important goals—climbing a mountain, running a company well, being a good parent—rarely do it by accident. Generally, those people are quite clear about what they want their future to be and stay focused on that hoped-for future through triumphs and tribulations, victories and mistakes. They are strategic in the most fundamental sense. They have a clear idea of what success would look and feel like for them, and it serves as a kind of operational North Star. They make decisions based on whether a particular choice will move them toward that desired future state. It may seem obvious, but I'll say it anyway: if you don't know where you're going, it's hard to know how to get there.

TOO MUCH OR NOT ENOUGH

Before I offer some guidance about how to envision the outcome you desire most clearly and usefully, let me share with you some common pitfalls of this process. I provide these as cautionary tales, so you know what to avoid in creating a vision that works for you.

IGNORING REALITY: One of the common mistakes people make in describing the future they hope for themselves is to deny or gloss over their current reality. TV talent contests offer a particularly clear and poignant set of examples: young people absolutely committed to a vision of themselves as world-class singers or dancers, regardless of the fact that they have none of the required talent or skills! I see this pattern often (though less glaringly obvious) in the workplace: people who believe they can be promoted into jobs for which they're not well suited simply by virtue of a strong desire to have those jobs; others who envision their company as it could be and hold fast to that vision—regardless of the fact that senior people at the company don't share the vision and are unlikely to move in that direction.

The sad thing is that when these pie-in-the-sky visions don't come to pass, people tend to blame others or to blame visioning itself, saying some version of "I guess it just doesn't pay to have hopes and dreams" rather than focusing on their own faulty assessment of reality. This is one reason why, in thinking strategically, it's so critically important to get really clear about the "what is" before moving on to "what's the hope." Unless you can be a "Fair Witness" about where you're starting from and what you have to work with, it's all too easy to set your sights on an unreachable outcome.

SETTING THE BAR TOO LOW: Some people are hamstrung in exactly the opposite way. For whatever reason—lack of confidence in their own ability, a dearth of examples in their lives of people who have achieved important goals, fear of failure—these people hesitate to envision a hoped-for future much different from what they have now. Just recently, I was having an on-line conversation with a group of people. We were talking about how to avoid getting burned out at work, and I noted that people who enjoy what they do report much less work-related stress than people who don't. One of the women involved in the conversation—a person who doesn't really enjoy her job and often agonizes about whether she should be doing something else—replied that most people don't like their jobs and can't do much about it. I thought about how powerfully she had imprisoned herself by holding that belief. By believing that most people don't like their work and *can't do much about it*, she makes it seem logical to believe that she will only be setting herself up for frustration and disappointment by envisioning some future where she's doing work she truly enjoys.

REASONABLE ASPIRATION

The process I'm discussing—the process of being strategic—provides a way to overcome both these limitations. Starting from a clear and balanced sense of "what is" and then doing what I call envisioning the hoped-for future is a powerful technique for engaging your brain's ability to imagine new realities while overcoming your brain's almost equally strong ability to generate reasons why a new reality isn't feasible. Here's how it works.

ENVISION THE HOPED-FOR FUTURE

Pick a time frame for success
Imagine yourself in that future
Describe what success looks and feels like
Select the key elements

PICK A TIME FRAME FOR SUCCESS: First, decide on a reasonable time frame for success. In some cases, this may already be determined—for instance, a large project that has a built-in deadline. In other situations, you may have to make your best guess. If you're envisioning the hoped-for future of the department you manage, you might pick a date one or two years out to allow time for making substantive changes in people or processes. If you're envisioning a larger undertaking, such as starting a business or a family or changing your career, you might want to pick a date three or four years in the future.

IMAGINE YOURSELF IN THAT FUTURE: This, as I noted earlier, is the critical step in this part of the process. To overcome your mind's resistance to letting go of current limitations, you need to create a three-dimensional piece of "possible future." Put yourself into a mental time machine. Then, when you emerge, imagine that you're sitting in the same room, in the same chair, but it's now the date you chose earlier: you've returned to this room, this chair, to celebrate the fact that you've addressed your challenge. It helps if you support your envisioning with a statement: "It's now January 19, 20__, and I'm reflecting on my success in addressing my challenge." Once you feel comfortably settled—in your imagination—in this future date, go on to the next step.

DESCRIBE WHAT SUCCESS LOOKS AND FEELS LIKE: As you mentally look around this new world at the end of your time travels, what do you see? Think about key events, feelings, circumstances, and outcomes that indicate to you that you've successfully created the future you want relative to your challenge. If you're envisioning the successful future of your department, you might want to focus on some of the following: the results you're getting; what it's like to work in the department, both how it feels and how things actually happen; what other people see (and say) when they look at or interact with you and your team; and how you're fulfilling your role as the leader. (Some people like to simply visualize these things, while others find it helpful to jot down their thoughts.)

SELECT THE KEY ELEMENTS: When you feel as though you have a fairly robust picture of this future you want, select and write down the key elements—those parts of the future that are key to your vision of success. As with the "what is," you're sorting for impact. It helps to write down the handful of things you feel are the most critical indicators of the future you want to create. You can do this in a couple of ways. Some people simply review their thinking and write down those elements that are most important to them. You might have imagined there would be a better coffee machine in the break room, but that's not as important to you as your vision of your team consistently sharing important information with one another. Some people like to look for patterns and group the elements they've envisioned into key categories.

Try It Out

Now we're going to try this out. I suggest you just keep going with the challenge you've defined and for which you clarified the "what is" over the past two chapters. (If you'd like to use another topic, that's fine, too. Just be sure to take a few minutes before you start the following activity to clearly define the new challenge and then do some quick, Fair-Witness-with-the-camera-pulled-back assessment of the "what is." If you don't do these two initial steps, you may have a hard time clearly envisioning your hoped-for future.)

✓ **PICK A TIME FRAME FOR SUCCESS**: Pick a point (a specific date) in the future that will allow you to have made substantive progress toward addressing your challenge but that's not so far away it will be difficult to envision accurately (two to three years versus twenty years, for example). Write your selected date below:

_____

✓ **IMAGINE YOURSELF IN THAT FUTURE**: Same room, same chair, same book—but it's the date you've selected above. Really let your mind get into the idea that you're now in that future date. (You might want to reinforce this by saying aloud, in the present tense, a few things that will have happened by that date: "my son has finished middle school" or "my sister turned forty last year.")

✓ **DESCRIBE WHAT SUCCESS LOOKS AND FEELS LIKE**: When you feel firmly grounded in this future date, think about how your challenge has been addressed. What's happening? How does it feel? How does it look, to you and others? In answering these questions, you can simply close your eyes and imagine, or you may want to jot down your thoughts here or on another piece of paper.

✓ **SELECT THE KEY ELEMENTS**: Review what you've written here or what you've thought through and capture the four to seven aspects of your vision that are most important to you. Write them below. You can either select the ideas that best capture for you the key elements of your hoped-for future or group your ideas into categories and name the categories.

WHAT'S THE HOPE: REASONABLE ASPIRATION

AN EXAMPLE

Voilà! Your hoped-for future. You've now described for your-self the most important indicators that will let you know you've addressed your challenge. Now, you may not have ac-tually done the preceding activity. You may be the sort that reads through the "to dos" and comes back to them later, or you may feel as though you're not yet quite clear about how to do this. To help clarify how this works and—I hope—inspire you to try it yourself if you haven't yet done so, I've included an example here, based on a real series of conversations I had with a coaching client a number of years ago.

First, the background:

HIS CHALLENGE: "How can I get a job running something, versus being the number two person?"

HIS "WHAT IS": Positives: He had lots of experience as a head of operations and a manager. People liked working for him and he was good at organizing people and processes. He had skills and connections in a growth industry where there were lots of jobs. Negatives: He had never been the president or CEO of a division or company. Though people saw him as a skilled manager and operator, he wasn't necessarily viewed as a strong or visionary leader.

Here's how he worked through the "Envisioning the Hoped-for Future" activity (he and I did this activity together in March of 2001). I've reproduced the activity here in just the same way I outlined it for you earlier; his responses are in italics:

✓ **PICK A TIME FRAME FOR SUCCESS**: Pick a point (a specific date) in the future that will allow you to have made substantive progress toward addressing your challenge but that's not so far away it will be difficult to envision accurately (two to three years versus twenty years, for example). Write your selected date below:

<u>_____ *March 21, 2003* _____</u>

✓ **IMAGINE YOURSELF IN THAT FUTURE**: Same room, same chair, same book—but it's the date you've selected earlier. Really let your mind get into the idea that you're now in that future date. (You might want to reinforce this by saying aloud, in the present tense, a few things that will have happened by that date: "my son has finished middle school" or "my sister turned forty last year.")

✓ **DESCRIBE WHAT SUCCESS LOOKS AND FEELS LIKE**: When you feel firmly grounded in this future date, think about how your challenge has been addressed. What's happening? How does it feel? How does it look, to you and others? In answering these questions, you can simply close your eyes and imagine, or you may want to jot down your thoughts here, or on another piece of paper.

> *I'm division head in a large company, or running a smaller company*
>
> *Great fit for my skills—they need what I'm good at*
>
> *Well-run, well-respected organization*
>
> *In media or a related industry*
>
> *I have the support of senior management*
>
> *There's clear accountability and authority*
>
> *I've built a great team*
>
> *We're getting consistently good results*
>
> *Creating new stuff—systems, approaches*
>
> *People see us as being state-of-the-art in what we do*
>
> *I'm up for the challenge*

I get along well with my peers

I'm enjoying work

People see me as a leader

My team works hard and has fun

Lots of results-oriented collaboration

✓ **SELECT THE KEY ELEMENTS:** Review what you've written here, or what you've thought through, and capture the four to seven aspects of your vision that are most important to you. Write them below. You can either select the ideas that best capture for you the key elements of your hoped-for future or group your ideas into categories and name the categories.

I'm the leader—and it's working

A team that fires on all cylinders

Highest-quality company and products/services

Good times getting excellent results

You can see that he collected his list of descriptions about his future into four "headline" statements. This became his internal memory device for the future he envisioned. In fact, he wrote them on a card that he carried with him in his wallet.

By the way, my client achieved his hoped-for future, running a major division within a large media company. He created a team that, for the most part, worked really well together, and they got the best results of any division in the company for three years running.

In Real Life:

To make envisioning your future a normal part of how you operate, it's important to find out if you tend to dream too high or too low, so that you can recalibrate. Here's a quick exercise to find out if you tend to fall into either of these traps:

Spend two minutes thinking about where your life will be in five years. Ready? Now, which of the following most closely describes your thinking process:

    a. I'm going to be living the life of my dreams; nothing can stop me.

    b. I've got some important goals, and I believe I can achieve them.

    c. I don't believe in planning; I just let life unfold.

    d. I don't think much will change.

If you answered "a," you may be "dreaming too high"—make sure you have a clear grasp of your "what is." If you answered "c" or "d," you may be "dreaming too low." You can use the approach in this chapter to open up your thinking about what's possible. If you answered "b," go for it!

FIVE

What's in the Way: Facing the Facts

"I could throttle that man," Llewellyn grumbles, throwing himself into a chair by the fire and glowering at the flames.

"Who?" asks Joan, his wife, calmly taking his cloak and nodding to a servant to fetch some mulled wine.

"That bullheaded Gryffudd. He's convinced we're not going to be able to get the stone we need for this castle up the hill. He thinks we should just forget about building it from stone and make the same kind of wooden hill fort we've been building for hundreds of years." He slaps his gloves against the arm of his chair. "I know it's going to be a hard job, no doubt of that. But why must the old fool try to talk us out of it before we've begun?"

"Mmmm," Joan responds, pouring the hot wine.

"And then Huw," he continues. "God love that lad, but he's just the opposite. Refuses to think about all the potential problems, just wants to get started." He takes the mug of wine and relaxes against the chair's high back, sighing. "Thanks,

my love," he says. "Between the two of them, they're driving me mad."

Joan pats his shoulder and then sits on a padded bench next to his chair. She looks into the fire for a few moments while he sips his wine. "Maybe," she says slowly, "maybe you need to bring everyone together and just get all the difficulties out at once. Tell them to say what could get in the way; then you can plan for how to overcome it." She's warming to her idea now, and turns to Llewellyn. "Only let them talk about what the obstacles are, not what to do about them—that should help with Gryffudd. And Huw can just cool his heels and listen."

Llewellyn nods, smiling. "Joan, I swear you're worth any ten of them. It's true we need to be realistic about what could prevent us from building this castle. We just can't let those difficulties stop us. I'm convinced more than ever that having a strong castle on the promontory is the best way to protect this part of the coast."

TROLLS UNDER THE BRIDGE

So, let's recap. You have an important challenge you're thinking about (for instance, how to solve a problem with a co-worker, or determining the kind of department you want to create), and you're thinking about it strategically. You've assessed your current situation by being a Fair Witness, "pulling back the camera," and sorting for impact to help make sure you're looking at the most relevant information. You feel as though you now have a reasonably clear, balanced, and complete sense of your current reality relative to this situation.

This is where you're starting from. Think of it as point A. Then, you've looked ahead, picking a point in time that makes sense, and you've clarified the future you want to create. That's point B.

Now, there's one more task to complete before you roll up your mental sleeves and figure out how to get from point A to point B: identifying the potential obstacles. On the road from where you're starting to where you want to go, these obstacles are the "trolls under the bridge." If you ignore them, they'll eat you, and you have to get past them to arrive at your destination.

People often resist this step, because they're afraid it will be demoralizing and that they'll lose their momentum. (As you may have noticed earlier, Llewellyn's friend Huw falls into this camp.) To keep yourself from getting overwhelmed by the obstacles, it helps to frame them as "the things we need to overcome in order to succeed" versus "the things that are going to keep us from succeeding."

With that as your mind-set, how can you then make sure you're being clear-eyed and accurate about the obstacles? I suggest you use exactly the same approaches you used during the "what is" step:

FACING "WHAT'S IN THE WAY"

Be a "Fair Witness"
Pull back the camera
Sort for impact

BE A FAIR WITNESS (AGAIN): Your skills as a Fair Witness will really be put to the test in this step. Depending on your own particular wiring, you may tend to avoid looking at the obstacles (like Huw) or you may over-balance in the opposite direction and become completely paralyzed by them (like Gryffudd). The art here is to learn to look at obstacles simply as data. I'll help by teaching you a skill for managing how you talk to yourself about obstacles.

PULL BACK THE CAMERA (AGAIN): In this part of the process, you pull back the camera far enough to see both point A (the "What is?") and point B (the hoped-for future), and then think about the circumstances, events, or beliefs that could make it more difficult to get from point A to point B. You look at obstacles within you, as well as those outside of you.

SORT FOR IMPACT (AGAIN): At this point, sorting for impact is simpler than it was at first. Knowing where you're trying to go makes it easier to see what might get in the way. One way to sort for impact: Once you've pulled back your camera and generated a list of possible obstacles, go back and prioritize the list in terms of "derailment potential," noting those obstacles that you feel might pose the greatest threat to the achievement of your vision. I'll give you a chance to do this later in the chapter.

AN AID TO FAIR WITNESSING: MANAGING YOUR SELF-TALK

One thing that most hinders people from being strategic, I observe, is their difficulty in being a Fair Witness. I started talking about Fair Witnessing in chapter 3, as an important part of looking at current reality. In this chapter I'll explore Fair Witnessing more thoroughly, because I find it's even more difficult for most people to be truly objective about the obstacles to their vision than about their current situation— and I want to offer you the most help in the hardest part.

Being a Fair Witness is a mental skill. It requires being able to observe and report without a lot of interpretation. Most people's mental monologue (self-talk) is a continual jumble of commentary, some of which is pure reporting (*this sweater is too small for me*) and some of which is highly interpretive and judgmental (*I look horrible and fat in this tight sweater*). We tend not to make a distinction between the two. We treat our interpretations and judgments as fact. All our self-talk has equal legitimacy for us, and Fair Witnessing goes out the window.

In order to disentangle this, let's start by looking at the point in any thought process (not just looking at obstacles) where we tend to drift into interpretation and judgment. Here's a little graphic you may remember from a college psychology class:

STIMULUS
↓
RESPONSE

Something happens. We respond. We tend to think that our response is pre-determined: "That guy insulted my mom. I have to smack him." What we generally fail to recognize is that something happens in between the stimulus and the response, faster than the eye can see: our interpretation of the stimulus. And that interpretation most often happens in the form of us talking to ourselves about the stimulus.

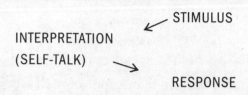

INTERPRETATION
(SELF-TALK)

STIMULUS

RESPONSE

Here's how it works. Stimulus: "That guy insulted my mom" (instantaneous internal interpretation: *That's an unacceptable affront to my dignity and merits a violent response*). Response: "I have to smack him." But you don't actually *have* to smack him. There are thousands of other possible interpretations of that stimulus, most of which would lead to different responses. For example: "That guy insulted my mom [*what a jerk; I don't need friends like that*]. I'll ignore him and not hang out with him anymore." Or "That guy insulted my mom [*boy, he's got her number, she really is a piece of work*]. Let's have another beer."

Now, the extremely good news is: you can control your self-talk—those little italicized phrases in the preceding paragraph that determine the response. You can bring them to your conscious awareness and change them, to produce a different response. For instance, when you're trying to approach a situation more strategically, you can use this skill of managing your self-talk to create a more accurate and open response to the obstacles before you: to be a better "Fair Witness." Let me walk you through how to gain more control over your self-talk; then we'll apply it to the process of looking at obstacles.

—————— MANAGING YOUR SELF-TALK ——————

Recognize

Record

Revise

Repeat

RECOGNIZE: The first step in managing your self-talk is to "hear" it. Mostly our little interior commentator runs and runs without our even being consciously aware that we're talking to ourselves, much less what it is that we're saying. Unless you're aware of this internal monologue, it's impossible to change it. So, the first step in this process consists quite simply of recognizing what you're saying to yourself. For instance, in thinking about obstacles, you might hear your mental voice saying, *I don't need to think about difficulties—that will be a bummer—I'll just keep going.* Or your particular self-talk might be exactly the opposite: *Yeah, there are all kinds of reasons this won't happen. I should just give up.* Once you start listening for them, you might be very surprised at the messages you're sending yourself.

RECORD: Writing down your self-talk is an important part of managing it, particularly if it's something you've said to yourself habitually over a long period of time. Recording it, on paper or electronically, creates a useful separation. When you can see it written down, your internal monologue no longer feels so much like an intrinsic part of you. (Maybe it's something like getting your hair cut or losing a tooth.) Let's say you write down that second self-talk statement above: *Yeah, there are all kinds of reasons this won't happen. I should just give up.* Having written it down, you might look at those words and think, "That's *what I've been telling myself? Yikes!* Once you recognize and record it, you'll also be better able to look objectively at the negative responses created by this self-talk: abandoning goals that are important to you, perhaps, or feeling cynical or hopeless about the possibility of changing a bad situation.

REVISE: After you've recorded your unhelpful, inaccurate, or unsupportive self-talk, you can decide how to "rethink" it. This step is the core of the process. You want to create alternative self-talk that you'll *believe* and that will lead to a more appropriate response. For instance, if you try to substitute self-talk that feels falsely positive to you, like *There's no reason I can't do whatever I want,* you simply won't believe it and therefore it will have no impact on you. What could you say to yourself instead that's believable and that would create a more useful response? How about something like: *I know there are reasons this might not work. I'll look at them carefully, so I have the best chance of understanding and overcoming them.*

REPEAT: Like changing any habit, managing your self-talk requires repetition. Substituting more hopeful and accurate self-talk for your negative self-talk will be helpful the very first time you do it. *And* you'll need to consciously do it again the next time the voice in your head comes up with a similarly negative statement. And again. You're creating new habits of thought. Whenever you find yourself falling into a pattern of negative self-talk, consciously substitute your revised, more hopeful and accurate self-talk.

Try It: Recognizing Your Self-Talk

At this point, I want to you to put the book down and try an experiment. Go about your normal life for the next thirty minutes or so and focus on listening to your self-talk—all of it: positive, negative, or neutral. You don't need to judge, categorize, or change it—just get conscious about what you're saying to yourself and note how this internal monologue affects you, both how you behave and how you feel. Then come back and we'll take a look at what you found out.

OK? See you later. . . .

Now, note in the following space some of the things you discovered you were saying to yourself, both positive and negative, and the impact they had on you: how your self-talk prompted a response, either behavioral or emotional.

What I Said to Myself	How I Felt/Acted as a Result

Try It: Managing Your Self-Talk

Now I invite you to try the model, using one of your own self-talk statements from the preceding page.

✓ Choose a self-talk statement that prompted a response from you that you didn't like or find helpful. Record it here:

✓ Write revised self-talk that you could use in this situation, self-talk that you believe and that will have a more positive outcome:

✓ Finally, note a few ideas for "repeating"—for making this rethought self-talk a new mental habit:

I'm a huge fan of this approach to managing my self-talk. It's helped me to stay focused when faced with stressful or difficult circumstances. It's also given me a way to let go of limiting or negative beliefs about myself and others and to be much more objective in looking at current reality and at obstacles—which really supports me in being strategic.

Here's an example. A few years ago, I was having my year-end "feedback wrap-up" session with my assistant, Anne, where she and I give each other feedback about things that are going well and ways we can improve. She told me she sometimes found it hard to give me bad news because rather than just taking it in, I tried to talk her out of it. I made an effort to convince her that the problem didn't really exist or show her how the situation was better than she thought it was. As soon as she said this, I realized she was right. When it comes to clients' problems, I get very interested and really want to explore the situation to help them understand and solve them, but I wasn't reacting the same way to problems in my own company. When I investigated my self-talk around those situations, it was something along the lines of; *Anne always thinks things are much worse than they are. If I listened to her, I'd get completely bummed out and stuck.* Pretty poor self-talk: neither true nor helpful.

So I committed to Anne to be more receptive in the future, and my revised self-talk was: *I need to get curious about what she's saying. She may be seeing this situation more clearly than I am. If there really is a problem, I won't be able to work on solving it unless I know what it is.*

So far, so good. My response is changing, and now I'm in

the "repeat" phase—continuing to consciously substitute my new self-talk when somebody tells me about an obstacle within my own organization.

BACK TO BEING STRATEGIC: FACING "WHAT'S IN THE WAY"

Let's return to our larger focus on the whole "looking at the obstacles" part of being strategic, incorporating what you've just learned about managing your self-talk. Here's the model again:

——————————— **FACING WHAT'S IN THE WAY"** ———————————

Be a "Fair Witness"

Pull back the camera

Sort for impact

Just as I have in previous chapters, I'm going to give you a chance to apply this part of the process to the challenge you defined for yourself.

Try It Out

Turn back to the vision you created in the last chapter (it's on p. 65) just to remind yourself of your thinking so far. You can write the key elements of your vision here, if you don't want to keep turning back to look at them:

Key elements of my hoped-for future:

✓ **BECOME A FAIR WITNESS**: Before you begin thinking about the obstacles to achieving your vision, become conscious of any unhelpful self-talk you may have, either about looking at obstacles in general or about specific obstacles that you may be either resisting or over-emphasizing. Pick out the one or two self-talk statements you think could make it hardest for you to be a Fair Witness in looking at the obstacles to your vision. Below, Record and Revise them:

✓ Record:

✓ Revise:

✓ **PULL BACK THE CAMERA:** Now, with your "Fair Witness" self-talk in place, you'll think about the obstacles to your vision. Mentally "pull the camera back" so that you can see the whole picture: where you're starting from and where you're trying to go. What's likely to get in the way? That is, what difficulties, constraints, or challenges are you going to have to get over, around, or through in order to move from where you are now to your vision of the future? I've found it's most valuable to look at both the obstacles outside you (in your company, with other people, etc.) and the obstacles within you (lack of skill or resource, self-doubt, etc.) Using your "Fair Witness" self-talk to keep yourself honest and balanced, feel free to use the following chart to jot down your thoughts:

Obstacles Outside Me	Obstacles Within Me

✓ **SORT FOR IMPACT:** Review what you've written and circle those obstacles you believe have the highest potential to derail you from moving toward your vision and that therefore are most essential for you to overcome.

How It Actually Works

Here's an example of how looking at obstacles in this way can support being truly strategic. Recently I was facilitating a meeting of a group of PR executives working within a larger media company. It was a yearly goal-setting session, focused on their individual business unit goals and on their goals as a department. One overall goal was to work together more effectively as a group. For example, they wanted to make sure they all were getting and relying on the same critical information about media sources. One person brought up a potential obstacle to achieving this. She noted that they were using a number of different outside data services, without discussing the information they were getting. The SVP who heads the department interrupted, saying, "Oh no, I think we're pretty clear about that. We all use the same two resources." I could almost see her self-talk; it was so similar to self-talk that I've had to work on changing. I imagined a thought bubble over her head, filled with anti-obstacle self-talk: *No, it's OK. Let's keep moving. This isn't a problem. It's already fixed. . . .*

I said, "Wait a sec; let's focus on this for just a minute. We may be able to solve this easily once we get a little more information." (This is pretty much the revised self-talk I use when my own internal monologue tries to stop me from looking at obstacles.) The SVP opened her mouth to respond, then closed it. She's a very smart and self-aware woman, and she immediately got what was happening.

We spent some time exploring this obstacle (it *was* a problem, but not an enormous one) and the other issues that were impeding their working together. After discussing the obstacles, the group agreed on which were the most important to address, and we were able to move on to "what's the path"—how they would overcome the obstacles in order to get from where they were to where they wanted to go. And that's the topic of the next chapter. . . .

In Real Life:

Think about a current situation in your life where you've stopped yourself from moving forward because you felt overwhelmed by the obstacles. OK, now take a few minutes to recognize, record, and revise your self-talk about the obstacles in this situation.

Then pull back the camera and look at the situation as though you're someone else: a neutral third party, a Fair Witness. As this other person, not you, note the starting point, the hoped-for future, and "what's in the way." As you observe the situation from this third-party vantage point, note any changes in your perception of the obstacles and their impact.

What's the Path: Roadway First, Then Asphalt

"And the men who'll be building won't be able to tend their fields or spend as much time hunting for their families," *Llewellyn finishes. He looks around the table. "So, any other potential difficulties?"*

The men glance at one another and shake their heads. They've spent the last few hours gathered around the council table in Llewellyn's main hall, talking through all the things that could get in the way of building a strong stone castle on the hill above Criccieth—one large enough to hold fighting men and supplies, easily defensible and a powerful point from which to attack. Llewellyn has kept them focused on just looking at the obstacles, rather than arguing what to do about them. Once Gryffudd let go of trying to convince them the whole idea was impossible, it felt to the rest of them like a worthwhile and practical thing to discuss.

Huw leans forward. "The women are strong hearted and

will want to support us in this," he says, responding to the final obstacle Llewellyn mentioned. "They can do much of the field work while the castle is being built, and—"

Ifor breaks in, "But hunting, Huw? Maybe we can keep a few of our best hunters aside from building and have them hunt for all of us. That way—"

Llewellyn stops them with a raised hand. "These are important considerations, but before we starting arguing over details, we need a plan."

"But that's what we're doing," Huw says, confused. "We're trying to plan for how to get enough food to carry us through while the castle is being built."

Llewellyn shakes his head. "I mean a plan for the whole enterprise." He spreads his arms wide. "If we can agree on the most important things we need to consider, then it will be easier to decide the details of how to make those things happen."

Gryffudd, who's been looking thoughtful during this exchange, now says, "I think I understand, my lord. Food is just a part of a bigger effort. We need to decide how to support and defend ourselves overall while the castle is being built."

Llewellyn slaps his palm on the council table. "Exactly!" he says, grinning. "That's exactly what I mean."

Once you've gotten clear about where you are and where you're trying to go—how you envision your "castle on the hill"—and you've gotten a reasonably good handle on what's in the way, it's a huge temptation to just starting running up the hill with tools in hand. Stop yourself! This particular point is the beating heart of being strategic. You have the opportunity here to select strategies that will form the core of your effort, instead of dissipating your hard-won clarity in a flurry of activity or, worse, a flurry of argument about which activities are best.

CORE DIRECTIONAL CHOICE

Let's go back to the definition of being strategic:

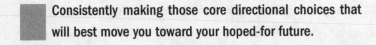

Consistently making those core directional choices that will best move you toward your hoped-for future.

That's what strategies are: core directional choices. And tactics are the specific actions you'll take to implement those core directional choices. Think about it this way. You're at point A and you want to get to point B. So you need to find a road that will get you from point A to point B, while getting around, over, or through the obstacles. Strategies are the road you choose—the path you'll take. Tactics are the road graders and asphalt you'll use to build that road.

Perhaps the best thing about having clear strategies is that they serve as an organizing principle for your tactics. There are—literally—thousands of tactical steps you could take to try to achieve any goal (as you began to see unfolding in the conversation at the beginning of the chapter), and without agreed-upon strategies, how will you choose among them? I can't tell you how many times I've watched groups of people argue over tactics because they don't have agreed-upon strategies to use as a screening mechanism.

Here's a great (and more recent) historical example of clear strategy, one that makes obvious the power of having those "core directional choices" as a frame for action.

STRATEGY FOR THE GREAT DEPRESSION

When Franklin Delano Roosevelt first ran for president in 1932, the United States was already cycling down into what would be the longest and most significant depression in its history. The sitting president, Herbert Hoover, seemed overwhelmed by circumstances and unable to frame any adequate response (for instance, he made speeches to business owners encouraging them "not to fire people").

FDR ran on a platform that envisioned a better future for Americans. His basic promise was that he would "get America back on its feet," a compelling hoped-for future for a country with a 25 percent unemployment rate! The current state was daunting: a struggling and under-insured banking system, faltering businesses, thousands losing their jobs daily, the weakest and least able members of society ill and hungry. The obstacles were daunting as well: failing banks and the weak stock market made people hesitate to invest. Those who were doing OK were worried more about their own ongoing security than helping others. The Federal Government wasn't set up to offer much support.

Once he was elected, FDR looked at the current state, his hoped-for future, and the existing obstacles and proposed the following three strategies for ending the depression and "getting America back on its feet":

- Get immediate help to those who need it most.
- Put people back to work (even if you have to "make it up").
- Work with our world partners to stabilize the economy.

Now, some historians argue that World War II ended the depression, not FDR's programs, but my point is simply that his are excellent examples of clear strategy. They define the *core directional choices* FDR and his administration agreed to make in order to move toward their desired outcome. Rather than describing specific actions, these strategies provided a *frame* for action. "Get immediate help to those who need it most" is not a specific thing you can run right out and do, but you can define the specific things that *would* implement that direction. Some examples of specific actions that were taken to implement that strategy: creating breadlines in major cities, funded by a combination of state and federal monies and donations from wealthy citizens; creating a program where medical students staffed emergency clinics as a way of paying part of their medical school tuition.

One of the most important things about strategy is that it helps you decide what *not* to do. Most businesses (and most individuals) waste a lot of time and effort focusing on doing things that won't necessarily move them toward their hoped-for future . . . they have no agreed-upon framework for "picking their shots," and so they tend to just default to doing what seems best at the time, or what people argue for most persuasively. If someone had come to FDR and said, "Let's create a program to raise money to save small-town movie theaters," he and his advisors could have used their strategies as a mechanism for deciding whether or not to do it: "Hmmm, getting immediate help to those who need it most? Putting people back to work? Working with our world partners to restabilize the economy? Not so much. Next!" (In fact, this did happen. Check the history books.) Clear strategy provides a framework for choosing the most effective tactics.

A WORD ABOUT TIME FRAMES

In the chapter on vision, I talked about setting a realistic time frame. Depending on the size and complexity of the undertaking on which you're focusing and the degree of change you're contemplating, your time frame for visioning might be anywhere from a year or so (reorganizing a small department or finding a new house) to three to five years (determining a company's future or radically changing your career path).

Strategy and tactics also have appropriate time frames. We've found, over the years, that twelve to eighteen months seems to be a workable time frame for creating strategies. After a year or so, it generally makes sense to come back to the strategies, see which ones you've completed, and see if the ones still being worked on remain the best core directional choices for moving toward your vision. You look at where you've come from, review where you're going, and decide whether the strategies you crafted are still the best way to get you there.

Tactics have an even shorter time frame. Usually four to eight months is best. There are two reasons for this. First, you don't want to bite off more than you can chew. You'll overwhelm yourself if you try to do detailed planning for the next two years! Second, it becomes a "confounded experiment," one where there are too many variables to draw clear conclusions. It's pretty much impossible to know enough about what will be happening two years from now to do realistic detail-level planning.

It's kind of like MapQuest. When you're looking at the "Region" level (vision), you can see for hundreds of miles; when you move to "City" level (strategy), it becomes dozens of miles; and when you come down to "Street" level (tactics), it's just a few square miles. The greater the level of detail, the smaller the area you can reasonably encompass.

LET'S DO IT, THEN

In the next two chapters, we'll explore how to craft powerful and directionally correct strategy and how to determine the tactics to best implement that strategy. First, let's clearly define both:

> **Strategy**: *core directional choices that will best move you toward your hoped-for future.*
> **Tactics**: *specific actions that will best implement your strategies.*

OK, so that's the basic premise of the "what's the path" step. We've reached the heart of being strategic. Let's explore it further.

In Real Life:

Over the next few days, simply note when people around you suggest strategies or tactics. Look for the distinction between "core directional choices" and "specific actions." Some places to look: meetings at work; politicians on television; parents talking about raising their kids. It's a great way to begin to recognize the differences between the two, and the different purposes they serve.

And, just for fun, here are some everyday examples of strategy versus tactics:

Dental hygiene versus prepping for the dentist:
Most kids brush their teeth when their parents make them or when they're going to the dentist (tactics). Most adults brush their teeth as a part of an overall effort at good dental hygiene (strategy).

Saving versus being a miser:
Some people save money in order to help them achieve a long-term goal, like home ownership or a college education (strategy). Some people just don't spend money because every time they think of buying something, they decide it's too expensive (tactics).

This quarter versus life of the business:
Some CEOs take actions in order to drive up the company's stock price short term, without thinking about the long-term consequences (tactics), while others act based on decisions they've made about how they want to grow the company long term (strategy).

SEVEN

The Art of Crafting Strategy

The dogs sleep under the table, having gotten all the scraps they can hold, and the men have pushed their chairs and benches back, replete, and are nursing their cups of mead.

They feel well pleased. After much discussion before and during the meal, they've agreed on the three most important choices they'll need to make in order to create the castle they've envisioned.

Llewellyn summarizes, "All right, my friends, we've made some important choices: we're all in agreement about the three parts of our plan. We need first to design the castle—a castle that will protect us as we hope, and that we can build with the skills and materials we have, or can get. Second, we need to decide how we'll build it—the whole process from start to finish. Third, we need to figure out how to defend and provision ourselves while it's being built. Is that about it?" He looks around the table.

Dafydd, who has perhaps had more to drink than most,

raises his cup. "Well done, my lord. I believe that is it: the best way to get from this room, dozing around the fire like old dogs, to sitting in our beautiful Welsh-built stone castle on the hill, dozing around the fire like old dogs."

Everyone laughs and raises their cups and mugs to Llewellyn, and to themselves.

The question "What's the best way to get from where I am to where I'm going?" is, in my mind, the essence of being strategic. It involves stopping your forward momentum, taking a breath, pulling back the camera (again), and reflecting on the core directional choices that will most effectively get you where you want to go. As I noted in the previous chapter, strategies are those "core directional choices" I've been talking about since the introduction. Crafting strategy is the process of determining which core directional efforts will *best* move you toward your hoped-for future.

As I noted in the last chapter, this is—ironically—the point at which people are most prone to *stop* being strategic. Even if they've stayed Fair Witness–like and thoughtful up till this point (clarifying their challenge, then understanding where they are, where they want to go, and what's in the way), this is where people tend—metaphorically—to jump up and just start climbing the hill. Or else to do the opposite: get overwhelmed by the seeming enormity of the distance to be crossed, shrug, and walk away.

So, I want to help you to avoid both those things. I want to help you learn to do the thing that most people fail to do at this point: craft strategy.

CRAFTING STRATEGY

Fortunately, the skills you've been honing throughout this process will serve you in this step as well. They provide a way for you to pull back from the confusion of tactics in order to first choose a clear strategic "road." Fortunately for you, the skills you've developed in previous parts of the process will continue to serve you here:

DETERMINING "WHAT'S THE PATH": STRATEGY

Be a "Fair Witness"

Pull back the camera

Sort for FIT

Be a "Fair Witness" and **Pull back the camera** are the same as they've been all along. You get as objective as possible and step back from the details to take in the whole picture of what you're trying to accomplish, so that you can select the strategies that will most effectively move you in the direction you want to go. The thing that's great about pulling back the camera at this point is that you can finally see the whole picture: where you are now, where you're trying to go, and what's in the way. It's like using the "Region" view on MapQuest to get driving directions from one city to another.

The principle behind **sorting for impact**—which you've used all along as a way to determine which things are most relevant—stays the same in this step, but we add some specifics about *how* to sort. The process we use to determine relevance in this final step is something we call **sorting for FIT**.

FIT AS A SCREEN FOR STRATEGY

Let me explain. "FIT" stands for "Feasibility," "Impact," and "Timeliness," and it's a great support for determining which strategies will *best* move you toward your desired outcomes:

Feasibility simply means deciding whether you can actually make a given effort. Do you have (or can you get) the resources, skills, time, and support you need to complete the strategy you're proposing? Is it possible, given the obstacles? (For example, our Welsh friends *could* have proposed as a strategy convincing the English to build the castle for them. Probably not feasible.)

Impact focuses on whether or not the proposed strategy is a good use of your resources. Will you get a "big bang for the buck"? In other words, will it give you a lot of movement toward your desired outcomes with a reasonable expenditure of effort?

Timeliness focuses on two things: ordinality (a great word, and one that I'm happy to have the opportunity to use here) and opportunity. "Ordinality" means the order in which things have to be done. Is this strategy something that needs to be done now, or are there other things that need to be done first? Opportunity is about having the chance to do something: is this strategy one that needs to be done quickly, before the window closes? Remember also that twelve to eighteen months is generally an appropriate time frame for crafting strategies. Focus on the strategies that make the most sense to accomplish in the next year to year and a half.

Let's walk through one of FDR's strategies as an example of using this "FIT" approach: **Put people back to work (even if you have to 'make it up').**"

Was it feasible? Yes, because Roosevelt had the resources of the Federal Government behind him, as well as the will of the U.S. electorate, which had just put him into office. He also had a huge group of out-of-work people who were ready and willing to do almost any sort of work to support themselves and their families.

Was it impactful? Yes, putting money into people's pockets for work done would have an immediate effect on all the businesses that supported working people. They and their families would once again be buying food and clothing, using transportation to go to work, getting their hair cut, buying school supplies, going to the doctor. It would set the wheels of commerce turning again and create a powerful positive shift toward "getting America back on its feet."

Was it timely? Yes: it needed to be done as soon as possible and was essential to put into motion before many other steps could be undertaken (steps that required people to be working, like collecting income tax). And there was opportunity. A great many large public works projects needed doing, given the dramatic shifts in the country's infrastructure with the advent of automobiles as a common form of transportation and electricity as the primary power source. Many thousands of people could be put to work building roads, dams, and hydroelectric plants.

You can see that this strategy passes the FIT test. If you ask the same three questions about his other two strategies, you'll see that they were FIT as well: core directional choices that would be feasible, impactful, and timely in moving the country from where it was toward where FDR had promised the American people it would go.

FIT is a useful screen for strategy because selecting good strategies is about "picking your shots." Think about it: success in any endeavor involves making good choices. Generally you don't have unlimited time or endless resources to devote to reaching a goal. You have to make the best use of the time and resources you do have. This is as true in business as in your personal life; I can't tell you how many times I've watched as business leaders squandered their energy on efforts that weren't FIT—that weren't best suited to helping them achieve their business goals. By being a Fair Witness, pulling back the camera, and then screening your proposed strategies with FIT, you'll have a great chance of making core directional choices that will get you where you're going, building your own business or personal castle on the hill.

Try It: Creating Strategy

Now you'll begin creating your own "path"—strategies for achieving the future you outlined in the previous chapters.

✓ Review your "what is" (p. 39), your hoped-for future (p. 65), and "what's in the way" (p. 80).

✓ Pull back the camera, so you can see all three elements in your mind's eye. (Remember the MapQuest metaphor!) If you like, you can summarize these first three elements of your situation below:

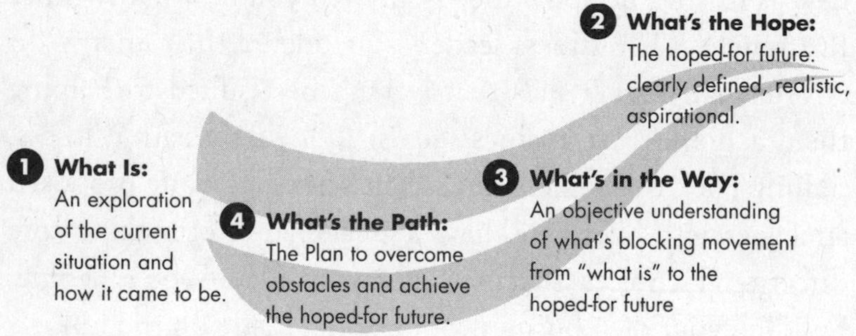

2 What's the Hope:
The hoped-for future: clearly defined, realistic, aspirational.

1 What Is:
An exploration of the current situation and how it came to be.

4 What's the Path:
The Plan to overcome obstacles and achieve the hoped-for future.

3 What's in the Way:
An objective understanding of what's blocking movement from "what is" to the hoped-for future

Figure 1

1. What Is

2. What's the Hope (Key Elements of Your Hoped-for Future)

3. What's in the Way

✓ Use the Fair Witness self-talk you created for yourself in chapter 5 to stay objective as you reflect on where you are, where you want to go, and "What's in the Way."

✓ Here, or on another piece of paper, propose possible strategies you'll use to achieve your vision:

4. What's the Path

✓ Now, "sort for FIT": check each strategy for feasibility, impact, and timeliness. Revise, eliminate, and/or add new strategies as necessary.

✓ Write your final three or four strategies below:

Strategies for Achieving My Vision in 20___

1.

2.

3.

4.

PERSONAL AND BUSINESS STRATEGIES

Before we move on to tactics, I'll share with you two examples of strategies for achieving a vision. The first set is personal. They're the strategies I devised when I was building my dream house last year—my own castle on the hill. The second are the strategies my client from chapter 4 created for achieving his vision of the career he wanted. In both cases, I'll also share the vision elements, so you have context for the strategies.

My Dream House, 2008 (for pictures of the completed dream house, go to www.beingstrategic.com)

> *Arts and Crafts farmhouse I design*
> *As "green" as possible*
> *Works for me now and for the future*
> *Beauty of the Hudson River Valley, without being too remote.*

My strategies for overcoming the obstacles and achieving my vision:

1. Explore alternative means of finding affordable land
2. Design the house I want
3. Create a team with an architect and a builder
4. "Bake" it into my personal financial plan

My Client's Dream Job, 2003

> *I'm the leader—and it's working*
> *A team that fires on all cylinders*

Highest-quality company and products/services
Good times getting excellent results

His strategies for overcoming the obstacles and achieving his vision:

1. Market myself to reflect my capabilities and passion.
2. Work with recruiters who understand and will partner with me to find what I want.
3. Focus on companies with the values that are important to me.

Good, solid pathways have been staked out. Now let's move on to talking about how to fill in those "core directional choices" with specific tactics in a way that will truly move you toward your vision . . . .

In Real Life:

Next time you're in a situation where people are trying to decide what to do about something, use your "what's the path" skills to suggest strategies instead of tactics. Some examples: deciding where to go on vacation, thinking about how to approach a big project at work, or helping a colleague solve a knotty interpersonal problem with a co-worker.

EIGHT

Tactics That Work

Llewellyn and Gryffudd stand on the castle site, facing north, where the promontory drops down toward the village and then the fields and woods beyond. Tremadog Bay glistens in the sun behind and below them, the sky above clearest blue chased with clouds. Gryffudd has spread out the plans on a hastily constructed camp table, with the edges held down by fist-sized rocks.

He points to the double gate-towers at the front of the drawing. "These are Hwyl's idea," he says. "He's been spying on the English fortifications near Shrewsbury, and had the thought that we could put a portcullis between them and be almost completely defensible."

Llewellyn squints, thinking. "And they'll be a good lookout to the north and east."

Gryffudd nods. "To the sea as well; they're the highest point between here and the mountains; we'll be able to see nearly to the end of the peninsula."

Llewellyn claps him on the shoulder, well pleased. "Work out with Hwyl the placement of the second curtain wall we sketched in; with that addition, I'll be content."

Gryffudd begins rolling up the plans, half-smiling. "You know, I never thought this would work."

Llewellyn laughs. "You made no secret of it."

"Well, you've changed my mind." Gryffudd says. "It's a good design, and the plans for building it and for defending and provisioning ourselves during the building are solid. . . ."

Clearly, Llewellyn's three strategies are providing useful organizing principles for the tactics that follow. And that, in a nutshell, is the beauty of defining strategy before creating tactics: Having directionally correct, FIT strategies gives you a *screen for action*.

WHAT'S THE ALTERNATIVE?

Just to demonstrate how unproductive and frustrating it can be to move to tactics before defining strategy, let me offer a present-day business example (one that I've created, based on a combination of clients). I've witnessed this all too often, and I suspect it won't be unfamiliar to you, either.

Ned Jameson, the CEO of greenbambino.com, the biggest on-line e-commerce site for natural baby products, has just de-cided that his company is missing a huge opportunity to define themselves as the primary authority on "greenness" for par-

ents. *He's tasked the Marketing and PR team with figuring out how to make that happen.*

Alicia Santos, the SVP of Marketing, has worked with her small team to review their current state and then clearly define how it would look if they were meeting that challenge. They've agreed upon a possible future, and they're excited about what they've envisioned. "OK," she says, turning away from the whiteboard. "So, we're saying that in eighteen months we want to be seen as the best source of information on the Web for 'all things green' for children under five. We want not only parents to see us that way, but our suppliers and the press as well. And we want our expertise to be seamlessly woven into our existing Web site, and to create new, related blogs or sites that provide more information and insight, reinforcing that perception for all our constituencies. Does that pretty much sum it up?"

Everyone nods or says yes.

"I know this amazing woman," Ella says, excited. "She's a mom of three small kids, and she has this great blog. One of her kids is in pre-school with my youngest, and I've gotten to know her pretty well. She's always finding new, cool baby products to turn people on to, and she reviews them in her blog. Maybe we can buy the rights to it and hire her part-time."

Alicia starts to respond, but another team member, Joel, jumps in. "You know, I'm not sure that's the right way to go. . . . Don't we need to make sure that we're connecting with people who are recognized experts—who have some track record in the natural baby business?"

"Yeah, I agree," adds Kumar. "How about if we talk to Joann, at Nature Child *magazine, and see if they want to hook up with us somehow? They definitely have the best reputation in the print realm . . . and their Web site is just starting to take off. Maybe we can do some kind of a joint venture that—"*

"Hey, you guys," Ella interrupts, a little irritated, "I think you dismissed my idea way too quickly. This person I'm talking about isn't just some hausfrau; she has a degree in early childhood education, and has been a leader in the community in terms of creating family-friendly public spaces—"

Joel says, "I'm sure she's great, Ella; I'm just trying to caution us against sacrificing substantive information for a nice vibe. If we really want to be the source of information on the Web—"

"But can't we do both?" asks Damian, the last and newest member of the team. "I mean, substantive and *friendly—"*

Kumar turns to him and says, "That's the beauty of Nature Child; *they—"*

Within moments, Ella and Joel's disagreement starts to escalate, Kumar is giving Damian in-depth background on the history of Nature Child, *and Alicia is wondering just when she lost control of the meeting. . . .*

This is a sadly common version of what tends to ensue when you try to go straight from vision to tactics: chaos.

But, thank goodness, you already know how to avoid this pitfall. Unlike poor Alicia, you know how to move smoothly from vision, to obstacles, to strategy—setting the stage beautifully for a far more focused and productive conversation about tactics. You can apply the definitions I've proposed for "strategy" and "tactics":

> **Strategy:** *core directional choices that will best move you toward your hoped-for future.*
> **Tactics:** *specific actions that will best implement your strategies.*

Let's rewind the tape and pretend Alicia has read the first seven chapters and that she's guided her folks through obstacles and strategies before opening the discussion up to tactics. What might that conversation sound like?

Ned Jameson, the CEO of greenbambino.com, the biggest online e-commerce site for natural baby products, has just decided that his company is missing a huge opportunity to define themselves as the primary authority on "greenness" for parents. He's tasked the Marketing and PR team with figuring out how to make that happen.

Alicia Santos, the SVP of Marketing, has worked with her small team to review their current state and then clearly define how it would look if they were meeting that challenge. They've agreed upon a clear hoped-for future, and they're excited about what they've envisioned. "OK," she says, turning away from the whiteboard. "So, we're saying that in eighteen months we want to be seen as the best source of information on the Web for 'all things green' for children under five. We want not only parents to see us that way, but our suppliers and the press as well. And we want our expertise to be seamlessly woven into our existing Web site, and to create new, related blogs or sites that provide more information and insight, reinforcing that perception for all our constituencies. Does that pretty much sum it up?"

Everyone nods or says yes.

Alicia turns back to the board. She's just read a new book called Being Strategic, *and she's trying out the approach it recommends. "Then we looked at the obstacles," she continues. "We had a lot of agreement there, so I won't go over them—and we've got four strategies we think will best support us in achieving our vision. Let me just reiterate those to make sure we're on the same page." She reads what she's written on the board:*

"'One: find out how we're now seen and what's wanted re "expertness" by our customers, suppliers, and the press.

"'Two: refocus our Web site toward "expertness," based on number one above.

"'Three: find and make agreements with additional outside experts who align with our brand.

"'Four: assure support for our plans by the rest of the senior team.'"

Alicia looks around at her team. "Is that it?" she asks. Again, they all nod. "OK, great. Then let's start creating tactics for the first strategy."

Damian, who's just been hired as the PR person, says, "How about if I take a crack at creating a draft questionnaire? I can make a basic one, and then we can tweak it, if we need to, for our three constituencies."

Alicia, writing Damian's name and the essence of the tac-

tic he's proposed, says, "I think that's a good place to start, Damian—when can you have that done by?"

Damian checks his PDA. "How about Friday?"

"Perfect," Alicia says, noting the date. "We can review and revise it in our staff meeting on Monday,"—writing that, too.

Ella, who's focused on consumer marketing, adds, "Then we can decide how to use the questionnaire to gather the info. I think we should do an online survey of the customers, with some incentive to respond, and maybe phone interviews with key suppliers and press contacts."

"That's great, Ella. Why don't you write up the approach you'd suggest and bring that to Monday's meeting as well?" Ella agrees, making a note to herself, and Alicia writes down the "who, what, and when" of this second tactic.

Joel says, "Don't we have to then create a time line for completing the questionnaires, doing the surveying and interviewing, and getting the information organized?"

Alicia nods, writing. "Let's agree to create that time line at the Monday meeting as well. Does that seem realistic?"

"I think so," Joel says. "I think we can sketch that out pretty quickly—and then we'll all be synced up."

"Do you want to make sure we remember to do that at the meeting, Joel?" Joel nods, and Alicia writes his name after the tactic.

Kumar, who has a strong background in statistical analysis, then says, "I'm happy to be the point person for sorting out what we get back from the surveys and interviews."

"How long do you think that will take?" Alicia asks, marker poised.

"Shouldn't take more than a couple of weeks from when we get the info," Kumar says. "Let's say I'll have an initial analysis three weeks after we finish collecting all the data."

"Good!" Alicia says, writing. "I sure don't want to do it."
Everybody laughs. "So, is that it for the first strategy?" she asks, pleased with her team's enthusiasm and clarity. . . .

Now we can walk away and let them finish creating their plan. They're well on their way.

This second scenario may seem unrealistically clear and straightforward, but I've actually seen it happen this way hundreds of times. Good strategy provides a marvelous "screen" for action, an organizing principle that allows you to fairly easily select those specific steps that will best help you implement a particular strategy. Without that organizing principle, as we saw in the first scenario, people tend to get mired into a welter of suggesting, defending, refuting, and countersuggesting: trying to decide which of the thousands of specific steps that could be taken should be taken.

And the same thing tends to happen when it's just you, creating an individual plan. . . . Strategy provides an organizing principle for the thousands of possible tactics running around inside your own head!

WHAT MAKES GOOD TACTICS?

I hope you're now persuaded that good tactical planning is best and most easily accomplished as a result of clear strategy. Let's talk, then, about how to create great tactics:

─── EXCELLENT TACTICS ───

Arise from strategy

Are FIT

Define what, who, and when

ARISE FROM STRATEGY: This is just a confirmation of all we've been talking about so far in the past few chapters. Rather than randomly suggesting and then performing actions that may or may not take you in the right direction (remember the tactical flailing in our first example), you define your strategies and then select the tactics that will allow you to best implement those strategies. I've found it's generally best to focus on one strategy at a time, as our example team did, fleshing out the handful of specific steps that will get you the most initial traction on one strategy before moving to the next.

ARE FIT: Just as when you're creating strategies, you continue to "screen" for feasibility, impact, and timeliness when selecting tactics. It may be even more important here, because you're focusing on practical action steps. This is where the rubber meets the road in terms of specific tasks you're committing to do in order to make your vision a reality. Ask yourself: Can I/we actually do this tactic, given current resources, skills and knowledge? Will it give me/us good "bang for the buck" in moving toward implementing this strategy? Should I/we do it now, or do other things need to be done first?

DEFINE WHAT, WHO, AND WHEN: At this point, you're finally *not* pulling back the camera. You want to see every detail, and it needs to be measurable. Agree on what the action is, who's going to be responsible for it, and when it will get done. In the preceding example, for instance, Damian is going to create a draft questionnaire for the group's review by Friday. Clear, simple, specific: everyone knows what is expected and will be able to tell whether or not it's been accomplished.

A FEW WORDS ABOUT "WHEN"

One thing I've noticed over the years as I've taught this approach is that people tend to be unrealistic about how long things will take to accomplish. It's easy to sit in a room, by yourself or with others, and set theoretical deadlines that don't take into account all the factors that can get in the way: others' conflicting agendas, delays in finding resources, waiting for others to make related decisions, even the fact that this plan won't be the only thing you have to do!

So, when you're establishing the "when" of your tactical plan, don't let your enthusiasm overwhelm you. Really think through what it will require to complete a tactic, especially given how other demands on your time may affect your ability to focus on doing it.

Remember also to select tactics that can be completed over the next four to eight months. As I mentioned in chapter 6, there are generally too many unknowns to plan further out than that and besides, you don't want to overwhelm yourself. You'll come back to your plan periodically and update it as you complete the tactics you've outlined at this beginning stage. (I'll talk about that in the next chapter.)

Try It: Selecting Tactics

Now (surprise, surprise) you'll have chance to do this yourself—here, you'll select tactics for the strategies you created in the last chapter.

✓ Review your strategies (p. 104); I suggest you rewrite them below for easier reference as you create your tactics.

✓ Now, create two to four tactics for each strategy.

Strategies and Tactics for Achieving My Vision in 20___

STRATEGY 1: Tactics		
WHAT	WHO	WHEN
STRATEGY 2: Tactics		
WHAT	WHO	WHEN

STRATEGY 3: Tactics		
WHAT	WHO	WHEN

STRATEGY 4: Tactics		
WHAT	WHO	WHEN

✓ Review your tactics. Do they arise from your strategies? Are they FIT in implementing your strategies? Is the "what, who, and when" clearly specified (and realistic!)? Revise them as needed.

THE PIECES ARE IN PLACE

We've traveled quite a distance over these last eight chapters, you and I: now you know the "how to" (and, perhaps more important, the "why") behind the model I shared with you at the beginning:

BEING STRATEGIC

Define the Challenge, then

Clarify *What Is*

Envision *What's the Hope*

Face *What's in the Way*

Determine *What's the Path*

Now you can approach any challenge in your life, simple or complex—from creating a better relationship with your boss to deciding where you and your family want to live; from helping your daughter get into the college of her choice to figuring out whether to go for your own graduate degree—more strategically, using the preceding model as a clear way of *consistently making those core directional choices that will best move you toward your hoped-for future.*

SO, WHAT'S NEXT?

In the following chapter, I'll share some ways of staying strategic. Once you've created your initial plan, it doesn't make sense to just rest on your laurels if you want to keep moving toward your hoped-for future, so I'll talk about how to keep moving forward. After that, in the last chapter of this first part of the book, I'll take you through this process with the focus being your own life: where the hoped-for future you're envisioning is the life you most want for yourself.

Then, in part 2, we'll expand our focus, and I'll share with you how to be strategic with a group: a collaborative approach for guiding others through this way of thinking about important challenges. I've used some "group" examples in this first part of the book (as with Alicia and her team in this chapter). In the second part, I'll teach you more about how to do it.

In Real Life:

Over the next few days, focus on honing your "what, who, and when" abilities. When you take on a task yourself or suggest a task to someone else, check to see whether it's clearly and measurably defined (will you know what "done" looks like?), it's clear who's responsible, and there's a clear (and realistic) deadline.

NINE

Building on Success

The Irish have been turned back with only one Welsh casualty; even the animals are safe, and no crops were lost. The newly built castle—the stonemasons' mortar barely dry—has clearly served its purpose.

Now the mead is flowing freely and every man, woman, and child from Criccieth and the surrounding areas is gathered in the castle courtyard, loudly toasting Llewellyn's health.

"To Life, to Gwynedd, to the Lord of all Gwynedd," bellows Owain, and everyone raises a mug or cup and echoes, "To the Lord of all Gwynedd!"

Llewellyn raises his cup back to them. "And to you all! Clear thinking, brave fighting, strong hearts!"

As everyone continues to rejoice in their good fortune and the proven strength of their new castle, Llewellyn turns to Gryffudd, Dafydd, and Huw, standing nearest him. "We're well served on the seaward side," he says, "but we need better defenses from enemies coming up the hill. We're just lucky the Irish weren't expecting what they got."

Owain, slightly the worse for drink, throws an arm around Llewellyn's shoulder and pours more mead from his own cup into his prince's. "Ah no, it's a brilliant castle, the best, couldn't be better," he crows.

Llewellyn gives Owain that level look of his. "It could be better," he says. "And it must be." He looks around the circle of men. "After the mead wears off tomorrow, we'll meet again in the hall." Suddenly he smiles. "Next time, we'll hand them their heads as they leave."

Laughing, they toast their prince yet again. . . .

STAYING STRATEGIC

I've been saying all along—and I'm saying it again—that being strategic isn't "a thing you do." It's not an isolated process that you undertake for an hour or a day and then put the results on a shelf and go back to your real life. To my way of thinking, being strategic means (all together now) *consistently making those core directional choices that will best move you toward your hoped-for future.* The word in that well-worn phrase that I want to pull out for you in this chapter is "consistently." It implies that if you want to keep moving toward the future you most desire, you need to stay focused on how to best do that. And life being what it is—never static, filled with variables and curveballs of all kinds—"how to best do that" is likely to change.

Fortunately, having read this far, you have the necessary tools: the mind-set and skills of being strategic that you've honed over the last eight chapters. As you continue moving forward toward a particular "castle," you'll simply apply these skills in a slightly different way. You'll reassess the "what is," reaffirm the hope, look to see whether "what's in the way" has changed, and refine or revise the path as necessary. In this chapter, I'll walk you through how to do just that.

HOMING DEVICES

I think of this process as "repositioning." It's like the recalibration that takes place in anything with a homing device, like a guided missile or the GPS system in a car. Imagine you're using your GPS to drive somewhere and you encounter a detour that you have to take. Your GPS will quickly recalibrate where you are relative to your destination and give you a new set of instructions that will keep you headed in the right direction, given your changed circumstances. In effect, your GPS continually updates where you are ("what is"), where you're going ("what's the hope"), and any obstacles, such as one-way streets or bodies of water ("what's in the way"), and offers you a new path. That's the process we're going to focus on in this chapter.

And, as you might suspect by this time, there's a model (which will look oddly familiar to you):

———————————— **STRATEGIC REPOSITIONING** ————————————

Refresh *What Is Now*

Reconfirm *the Hope*

Reassess *What's in the Way*

Revise *the Path*

REFRESH *WHAT IS NOW:* The point of this first part of repositioning (as in the GPS example) is to find out where you are *now*. You'll look to see if any important aspects of your situation or the conditions around you have changed. (For instance, I found out about some newly available "green" materials I could use in my "green as possible" house design. The client I was coaching toward his dream job discovered that a well-known media company was reorganizing in a way that created a job that might be a good fit for him.)

RECONFIRM *THE HOPE:* You need to make sure that your desired outcome is still the same. Most often, if you've been thoughtfully strategic up till now, your vision will remain essentially unchanged. However, occasionally as you move toward your vision of the future, you find that you've either overshot or undershot the mark in your visioning—been too aspirational or not aspirational enough—or you find that your vision isn't really what you most want after all. A close friend of mine, for instance, had envisioned building a good-sized consulting company, with a staff of consultants supporting him and delivering the work. But as he moved toward his vision, he realized that he didn't really want to put the time and effort necessary into building a team and managing people. He changed his vision to align more with his comfort zone of being a sole proprietor, operating within a network of loose relationships with fellow consultants.

REASSESS *WHAT'S IN THE WAY:* Very much like the first step, "Refresh *What Is Now*," here you're simply looking at how the obstacles may have changed since your initial planning (unforeseen resource constraints, for instance, or the loss of a strong advocate for your plan). Again, your Fair Witness skills will come in handy here—once you're moving forward it's all too easy to either underplay the obstacles (if you're the kind of person who just wants to keep moving) or overplay them (if you're a more cautious sort). In either case, unless you can stay reasonably objective, you're likely to react in ways that aren't useful.

REVISE *THE PATH:* Now you can use your updated view of "what is," the hope, and "what's in the way" to accurately revise your path, in order to assure that it's still those core directional efforts that will best move you toward your desired outcomes. You'll first review your strategies for FIT. They may stay exactly the same, or they may not: you may have completed one or more of them, and you may need to create new ones. Then you'll review your tactical plans. You'll be looking at whether you've done what you decided to do and what the results have been. In order to get the clarity you need, you'll be drawing upon your "Fair Witness" skills. You want to be balanced in your view of your efforts, as it's both distracting and counterproductive to be judgmental or blaming at this point. You may be ready for a whole new set of tactics for your existing strategies, and you'll also create tactics for any new strategies. Like your car's GPS, you're creating a new route for yourself. If no new obstacles have arisen and you're moving toward the same goal, it may not change much at all. If conditions have changed or you've altered your destination, your GPS may give you a very different path to follow.

And repeat. This review and reassessment becomes almost second nature as you begin to incorporate the art and practice of being strategic into your daily life. You'll fairly regularly find yourself looking to see what's changed and assessing whether you're still on track and, if not, what to do about it. It's how great leaders and successful folks in all endeavors keep themselves moving toward their goals.

AN EXAMPLE

Let's go back to our friends at greenbambino.com. As you may recall, Alicia Santos, the SVP of Marketing, is applying what she learned from reading *Being Strategic* to the challenge she and her team have been given by their CEO: How can they define themselves as the primary authority on "greenness" for parents?

> *It's been three months since Alicia and her team came up with their vision and strategy for "Operation 'We Know Green,'" as they've playfully dubbed it. They've been regularly checking in with one another on the progress of various tactics, and overall, it seems to be going well—but some things have changed, and Alicia decides to extend one of their weekly meetings and dedicate it to repositioning. (Since their initial meeting, she's finished reading* Being Strategic. *Part 2 gave her some useful tools for doing this with her group.)*
>
> *She's explained the basic premise to them—that they're going to do a more in-depth review of the plan and reposition themselves to keep moving forward effectively—but she decides to start the meeting by giving them a bit more context. Alicia*

greets Kumar, Damian, Ella, and Joel as they come in, and
when everyone is settled she begins. "So, basically," she says,
"I thought it would be a good idea for us to review our whole
plan and make sure we're still headed in the right direction."
Everyone nods, familiar with this idea from her pre-meeting
e-mail.

"Here's how I'd like to approach it," she continues. She's
written the repositioning steps on the whiteboard and points to
them as she explains. "First, we'll look at our current state
again. There may be conditions within us or around us that
have changed, and we want to factor that in.

"Next," Alicia says, "we'll look at our vision again, just
to confirm that we feel it still defines where we want to go. If
not, we can revise it." She points to the next step. "Then we'll
reassess the obstacles."

Kumar says, "That's a good idea—I'm a little worried
about ecokids.com; they've come up out of nowhere in the past
few months, and they're doing some very creative things."

"Exactly," says Alicia, turning to him. "That's exactly the
kind of thing I mean. We'll talk about that." She turns back
to the board and points out the next step. "After that, given
what we've understood, we'll look at where we are with the
plan: how it's going, whether we've done what we said we
were going to do. And if so, how is it working? If not, why
not?"

Alicia notices that Ella and Joel look a little worried at
this. She knows both of them tend to be concerned about being
perceived as "messing up." She continues, "I want to let you
know up front that the point here isn't to find out who's to
blame if something didn't happen. We're just trying to assess

really objectively what might have gotten in the way, so that if we still want to do that thing going forward, we'll have a better shot at it." Joel sits back in his seat, and Ella looks relieved.

"Then we'll revise our strategies and tactics as needed, to keep us moving from where we are now to where we want to go, given the current obstacles." She takes a deep breath. "Like Ecokids."

Let me pause for a minute here to laud Alicia for how she's set up this meeting. She's clearly integrated the model into her thinking. The idea of updating "what is, what's in the way, what's the hope, and what's the path" rolls right off her tongue. Of course, this is the beauty of being an author. You can create fictional characters who are wonderful learners and who do exactly as you would have them do! Nonetheless, it is possible to make the art of being strategic part of your approach to life, and that's what I'm trying to convey here.

Now, back to the meeting: I don't want to have you sit through the whole thing, so let's fast-forward a bit. When the group reviewed their current state, they realized not much had changed internally. The big change was the sudden growth of Ecokids, which they decided to explore in depth during the reassessment of obstacles.

They reconfirmed their vision just as it was: to be seen as the best source of information on the Web for "all things green" for children under five by parents, suppliers, and the press. They also wanted their expertise to be seamlessly woven into the existing Web site, with new, related blogs or sites that provided more information and insight, reinforcing that perception for all their constituencies. It still seemed like an accurate description of their "hoped-for future."

The big new obstacle was ecokids.com, which had been started by a major diaper manufacturer as a stand-alone project, but had both the deep pockets and the experienced staff of its parent company to draw upon. And it was definitely breathing down their necks. Let's jump back into the conversation:

> *Alicia turns back to the group, having just written down the essence of the Ecokids situation on the whiteboard. Everyone looks a bit somber. "Hey, guys," she says, "let's not bum ourselves out too much here. I'm confident we can overcome this potential obstacle. We have five years of customer loyalty they don't have, and let me remind you all of what Damian told us just last week: on the Web, it's not about money; it's about stickiness.*
>
> *"Let's revise our strategies and tactics, given where we are now, and given this new challenge." Everyone has gotten a handout with the four strategies; Alicia reads them aloud:*
>
> *" 'One: find out how we're now seen and what's wanted re "expertness" by our customers, suppliers, and the press.*
>
> *" 'Two: refocus our Web site toward 'expertness,' based on number one above.*
>
> *" 'Three: find and make agreements with additional outside experts who align with our brand.*
>
> *" 'Four: assure support for our plans by the rest of the senior team.' "*

Alicia looks around at her team. "So, what do you think?" she asks.

Damian, the PR guy, says, "Well, we've pretty much completed the first strategy. Should we take it off the list?"

Joel shakes his head. "I don't think so. I think we just need to revise it to make it ongoing. Like maybe 'stay in touch with our constituencies' current perceptions of and future needs/desires for our "expertness."'"

"That's good," says Ella. "And can we fold keeping our eye on Ecokids into that? Like maybe 'stay in touch with how our constituencies see us and what they want from us re "expertness," relative to our competitors.'"

Everybody nods, agreeing. "I like that," Kumar says. "That expands the strategy in an important way."

Alicia wipes out the old version and rewrites it as per Ella's suggestion.

As they continue to review their strategies, they decide to slightly revise the second one, to "continue to refocus our Web site toward 'expertness,' based on #1 above." They're mostly done creating the Web revision plan, but they want to make new tactics for implementing it and continuing to refresh it over time.

When they get to the third strategy, "find and make agreements with additional outside experts who align with our brand," Kumar says, "We've finished that one—at least the first pass. I wonder if we shouldn't incorporate the ongoing effort in this area into our second strategy?" When everyone looks a little puzzled, he continues. "Like, maybe the second strategy could be 'continually focus our Web site and other communication methods toward "expertness," based on number one above.' You know, so that it includes our new blogs, the e-newsletter we're talking about, our 'experts' making presentations. All that."

The others nod. "That's great," says Damian.

"Oooh, Kumar, you're so strategic," adds Ella, batting her eyelashes, and everybody laughs.

Alicia removes strategy 3 from the whiteboard and makes the recommended addition to strategy 2. "OK," she says. "What about number four?"

"Finito!" says Joel, a fist in the air. "Ned and the other partners signed off on the plans, budget and all, last Wednesday."

Everybody claps, and Alicia wipes it off the list. "So," she says, marker poised. "Any new strategies?"

"Yeah," says Kumar. "Ecokids. I know we've got some competitive analysis in the first strategy now, but I think they deserve their own strategy."

The rest of the group agree, and after some discussion they decide to create a new strategy 4: "get and stay clear about Ecokids, so we can build competitive responses into our own approach."

Alicia puts down the marker, satisfied. "All right," she says. "Let's take a break; then we'll do the tactics: remove the ones we've finished, eliminate or update the rest of the original ones, and then create new ones where we need them."

Damian says, "Can we start with number four? I'm itching to get to it—and it might inform our tactics for the other ones."

"Great idea," Alicia says. "Why don't you all come back in ten minutes and we'll start right in demolishing Ecokids."

Smiling and chatting, everybody heads for the door.

I'll leave the rest to your imagination. Suffice it to say they did a bang-up job of creating new tactics for their Ecokids strategy and updating the tactics for their other three. All five of them left the meeting feeling clearer (and better about their new competitive threat) and pretty proud of how much they'd accomplished in three months. They're approaching their work more strategically.

INDIVIDUAL REPOSITIONING

Though I've offered a group example because I thought it would be more fun and demonstrative, reviewing your strategic thinking by yourself is very similar to doing it with a group. It usually goes more quickly when it's just you, because there's generally less time needed for conversation (not always, though—some of us have *lots* of conversations going on inside our heads).

So, now I'll give you a chance to try it out. I suggest you read through the following section now, just to set it into your brain, then—at the end—make a date to come back to this section a few months from now and do it for real.

Try It Out

Here's a guide to "recalibrating" an initial plan. A few months after you've started working on the plan you created, come back and think through the following steps:

✓ **REFRESH *WHAT IS NOW*:** Look at your current situation (summarized on p. 102). Has anything changed? What impact is that having on you? Write below any important changes in your "what is."

✓ **RECONFIRM *THE HOPE*:** Review your hoped-for future (p. 103). Is it still a good description of your desired outcome? If not, note below how you'd like to change it.

✓ **REASSESS *WHAT'S IN THE WAY*:** Staying in Fair Witness mode, review the obstacles you surfaced at the beginning (p. 103) and think about whether they've changed: some may have disappeared, and new ones may have arisen. Be as objective as possible about the potential impact of any new challenges. You may want to write a summary below:

✓ **REVISE *THE PATH:*** Now review your tactical plan, on pp. 117 to 118. I suggest you make notes right on those pages about whether and to what extent you've done the things you decided to do. For things you haven't done, use your Fair Witness skills to reflect on what has gotten in your way and how you might overcome that going forward. Based on the understanding you've come to above, revise your strategies, and then your tactics, as appropriate, below.

My Revised Strategies and Tactics for Achieving My Vision in 20___

STRATEGY #1:		
Tactics:		
WHAT	WHO	WHEN
STRATEGY #2:		
Tactics:		
WHAT	WHO	WHEN

STRATEGY #3: Tactics:		
WHAT	WHO	WHEN

STRATEGY #4: Tactics:		
WHAT	WHO	WHEN

✓ Do a final review of your strategies and tactics, above. Are they FIT in responding to your "now" situation in order to keep moving toward your vision? Do they arise naturally out of the work you've done so far? If not, keep tweaking them: remember, you're trying to find the most realistic, efficient, and effective way to keep moving toward your hoped-for future.

STARTING TO GET THE MOVES

Just recently, my son-in-law was trying to teach me how to exercise using his Russian kettlebells. Without going into too much detail, it's an esoteric but extremely effective approach to physical rehabilitation and fitness using heavy metal balls with handles. He used them initially to recuperate from some sports injuries but now does it mostly because he likes it. When he first starting showing me how to do the most basic exercise, I felt like a klutz. I didn't quite get how to hold my body or the kettlebell or how to move. After a few minutes, though, it started to come together. Instead of feeling like I was doing a series of awkward and unconnected moves, I began to experience it as a unified "dance," a process.

I hope you're beginning to experience being strategic in the same way: as an integrated "dance" of steps that flow together into a unified way of seeing and responding to circumstances. If you're not quite there yet, don't worry about it. Keep playing with it, and it will fall together for you.

Before we turn our focus to the mind-set and mechanics of using this approach with a group, I want to give you one more chance to let the process settle into you. In this final chapter in the first part of the book, I'll invite you to use your newly honed strategic skills to focus on meeting a truly important challenge: getting the life you want.

In Real Life:

Try exercising your "recalibration" muscle. At work and at home, when looking at current projects, ask yourself two questions: "What's changed since I started this?" and "What might I need to do differently, in response to those changes, to complete this project successfully?"

TEN

The Castle of You

Llewellyn Fawr stands on a catwalk high inside the castle's southern curtain wall, facing the bay. He's alone for the moment; Gryffudd has gone to get the plans to see whether it would be possible to build more comfortable quarters for the guard inside the gatehouse towers.

There's a fresh breeze off the sea; Llewellyn's cloak billows about him, and his hair streams back from his forehead. The feel of wind on his skin, the sea's complex smell, and the stone beneath his hands, rough and warm, bring up in him a fierce joy. Now it's more than Gwynedd, *he thinks to himself.* We're creating a true Wales. These fractious Welsh lords of mine are becoming a single kingdom. *He thinks of the other castles: Dolbadarn, Dolwyddelan, Aberdyfi, Castell y Bere. Criccieth is the jewel in the crown, but he now has a network of castles throughout North Wales, intended to provide critical points of defense and attack.*

He knows his men are often puzzled by his actions, but

he sees it clearly: a future where Wales is united and strong, a country that can stand against the English, the Danes, the Irish—whoever might try to overcome them. Joan laughs, saying he's been touched for certain, but she's not sure it's by God. Nonetheless, he feels it is his destiny to create an independent Wales and then protect and defend it for his people.

In the introduction (and ever since), I've said over and over again that the skills and mind-set of being strategic are extraordinarily useful in every aspect of life, for challenges large and small, personal and professional. And both my own personal experience and my observation of others lead me to believe that being strategic is perhaps most valuable in the challenge that faces each of us: how can I create the life I most want for myself?

OTHERS ACHIEVING THEIR DREAMS

It's interesting, from this point of view, to look around me and notice others who seem to be living the lives they want. Some are famous; some are not. Some are wealthy; some are not. But I notice a few common characteristics: a quiet pride, a contentment, a sense of gratitude. I suppose I have an eye out for these people, and when I hear quotes that speak to me of an intentional and satisfying life I remember them. Here are just a few that have struck me recently:

"It doesn't matter who you are, where you come from. The ability to triumph begins with you. Always."

—Oprah Winfrey

"This opens up a whole new direction for my career, one that I've wanted. And my family is happy about it, too—this is really exciting."

—*a client, on becoming general manager of a cable television network*

"I'm just amazed to be here, you know? This life, this country. A dream for me since childhood."

—*A Pakistani cab driver in New York*

"Go confidently in the direction of your dreams. Live the life you have imagined."

—*Henry David Thoreau*

HOW ABOUT YOU?

So, I'd like to offer you a gift: the opportunity to be strategic about your own life, your own hoped-for future. Now, you may be that rare person who is already living the life of your dreams, and if so, you're welcome to go straight to the next chapter and begin learning about how to be strategic with a group. But if you'd like to explore this realm with me, let's get started.

As I said earlier, I'd like to propose the challenge for you in this chapter as:

"How can I create the life I most want for myself?"

Now, if you want to frame it differently or add some further refinements, be my guest. However, I just want to encourage you to focus on your life, rather than some smaller goal or project. If you've never done this before, it might seem a bit daunting, or even arrogant. Lots of people think it's unrealistic or over-reaching to try to say what they want in life and then go for it. I invite you to lay aside those concerns for the time being and simply try this out. What do you have to lose?

I don't mean that rhetorically. I mean it literally. If you've hesitated to clarify the future you want to create for yourself—for whatever reason—I invite you to ask yourself, "What do I have to lose by doing this? What bad consequences could arise from stating what I want in life?" I'll give you a minute to think about it.

OK, here are some of the most common responses to these questions:

- "I could fail; then I'd be disappointed or feel stupid."
- "I might change my mind."
- "People who matter to me might not be supportive."

All those things are definitely possible. I'd suggest you step back and become a Fair Witness of your life. All things considered, are those acceptable risks or not? In other words, is avoiding those outcomes more important to you than the possibility of achieving your hoped-for future? I'm encouraging you to weigh it consciously rather than allowing yourself to be automatically blocked by unexamined fears.

YOUR LIFE'S MAP

On the next few pages you'll find a template you can fill in as you work through this. I know you're familiar with the Being Strategic process by now, but just to refresh your memory as you focus on your life, I'll walk you through the steps as they apply to this challenge:

Try It: Your Hoped-for Future

✓ **CLARIFY WHAT IS:** First, you'll look at your current situation, as it relates to your challenge: "How can I create the life I most want for myself?" Where are you in your life right now—what's working and what isn't? What are your strengths and weaknesses? What supports you, and what doesn't? Be a Fair Witness, pull back the camera, and sort for impact.

✓ **ENVISION WHAT'S THE HOPE:** Given where you're starting from, what's the future you want to create for yourself? Pick a time frame, imagine yourself into it, describe what success would look and feel like, and select the key elements.

✓ **FACE WHAT'S IN THE WAY:** Pull back the camera to encompass the whole picture: where you are in your life and where you want to be. Now, being a Fair Witness (remember to manage your self-talk here) and sorting for impact, note the critical obstacles you'll need to overcome in order to achieve your vision.

✓ **DETERMINE WHAT'S THE PATH—STRATEGIES:** With the camera still pulled back, select those core directional efforts you want to make over the next twelve to eighteen months to move toward your envisioned future. Remember to sort for FIT.

✓ **DETERMINE WHAT'S THE PATH—TACTICS:** Now decide the specific actions you'll take to begin implementing those strategies over the next few months. Remember, again, to sort for FIT and define "what, who, and when."

THE CHALLENGE: *"How can I create the life I most want for myself?"*

WHAT IS	My Positives: Strengths, Skills, or Resources I Bring to This Challenge	My Negatives: Weaknesses, Challenges, or Lack of Resource I Bring to This Challenge
	Outside Positives: Things Around Me That Support My Addressing This Challenge	Outside Negatives: Things That Might Get in the Way of My Addressing This Challenge

WHAT'S THE HOPE

Time Frame:

Most Important Elements of My Hoped-for Future:

	Key Internal Obstacles to My Success (Within Me)	Key External Obstacles to My Success (Around Me)
WHAT'S IN THE WAY		

WHAT'S THE PATH—STRATEGIES	Strategy 1:
	Strategy 2:
	Strategy 3:
	Strategy 4:

WHAT'S THE PATH—TACTICS

What—	Who—	When—
Tactics for Strategy 1		
Tactics for Strategy 2		

What—	Who—	When—
Tactics for Strategy 3		
Tactics for Strategy 4		

WHAT'S THE PATH —TACTICS

SO, THAT'S IT

Now you know how to be strategic and why it matters. Like Llewellyn Fawr almost eight hundred years ago, you can build your own castle on the hill, whatever that castle may be, whatever the hill may be. You have a set of skills and a way of thinking that will allow you to consistently focus on making those core directional choices that will best move you toward your hoped-for future.

Now I want to offer you a whole new dimension for being strategic. We'll focus on how to invite others to be strategic with you.

In Real Life:

Since this chapter *is* your real life, I just want to give you one more tool to support your success in achieving the hoped-for future you've defined.

TURBO-CHARGE YOUR SELF-TALK

- Consider what worries you most about being strategic in approaching your own life.
- Imagine you have a kind and impartial "wise friend," a Fair Witness observing and advising you. What would he or she say to help you get past that worry, to assure it wouldn't sabotage your efforts?
- Write that advice below, and use it as supportive self-talk whenever your focus or your belief in your ability to achieve the life you want wavers:

PART TWO

BEING STRATEGIC WITH A GROUP

ELEVEN

Inviting Others Into the Process

L ast year I had the chance to revisit Criccieth Castle and was struck anew at the effort it must have taken to build. As I sat in the spring sunshine, chatting with my daughter (she loves Wales as I do, and we had decided to take a brief vacation, just the two of us, to reacquaint ourselves with its charms and so that I could do research for this book), I imagined long lines of thirteenth-century Welsh people hauling massive stones up the steep slope below us. Not just a few stones, mind you, but enough to build a whole castle. And I know enough about Welsh history, and how independent of spirit the Welsh have always been, to feel fairly certain that Llewellyn Fawr, their prince, had not compelled their labor through force or coercion. How did he get these people organized, focused, and committed to this huge undertaking?

That's what we'll explore in this second part of the book. It's one thing to decide to approach your own life and work strategically, but it's quite another to engage an entire group or enterprise in that process with you. Fortunately, you have a practical base of skills and understanding as your starting point. Everything I've discussed so far is applicable to being strategic with a larger group or team. In being strategic with a group, there are three additional things to think about: how to get people motivated to approach an issue or project strategically, how to modify the steps of the process to fully engage them in it, and how to guide a group through the process. In this chapter, I'll give you some insight into how to get people on board with the idea of using the process, and in the following chapters, I'll offer skills and approaches for conducting the process with them.

OFFERING THE POSSIBILITY

By this point in the book, if I've done my job well, you're feeling both capable of and reasonably enthusiastic about being strategic. My first job, as a catalyst for your learning, was to make you *aware* of the possibility of being strategic—of approaching opportunities and challenges in a new way. My second job was to help you see the benefits of being strategic; the ways in which this approach could help you personally, so that you would be *motivated* to learn these new ways of behaving and thinking. My next job was to share with you, simply and clearly, the *skills* of being strategic. And my final job was to guide you in *practicing* the skills in ways that would, again, be personally meaningful to you.

My colleagues and I at Proteus have refined this approach to learning over the years. Because it seems to work in most situations and provides a great map for how people learn, we've expressed it as a model we call LearningPath, shown in figure 2.

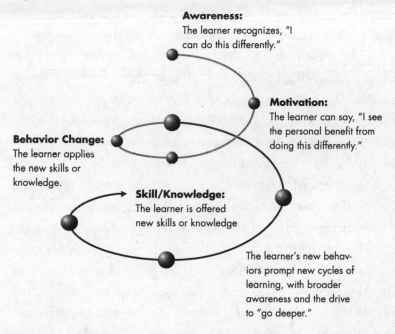

Awareness:
The learner recognizes, "I can do this differently."

Motivation:
The learner can say, "I see the personal benefit from doing this differently."

Behavior Change:
The learner applies the new skills or knowledge.

Skill/Knowledge:
The learner is offered new skills or knowledge

The learner's new behaviors prompt new cycles of learning, with broader awareness and the drive to "go deeper."

Figure 2

Very interesting, you may be saying to yourself, *but why is she telling me this?* It's because I'm recommending that you follow the first two steps of this path to invite the members of your group into the process of being strategic. Let's explore both steps in more depth.

AWARENESS

Think of the last time someone told you about something that really captured your attention, something you hadn't heard about before. Take a minute and recall an example.

If you're like most people, there were a couple of elements at play in this circumstance. First, you probably felt open to the person, and felt that his or her motivations were positive. Second, the person was most likely personally engaged with the thing. You sensed that he or she was endorsing it, not simply presenting information, and at the same time, he or she wasn't strident or insistent. It was more an offer of insight than a demand that you accept his or her point of view. Finally, the person probably provided examples or stories of the thing's efficacy, uniqueness, or value.

I experienced this recently. I was on vacation in Asheville, North Carolina, and I was getting a manicure. The polish I picked from the salon's selection was a brand I'd never heard of. The aesthetician, with whom I'd already made a nice connection—she was smart and funny and a really good listener—complimented me on my color choice and noted that this was a new brand she'd just started working with and that it was both lower in chemicals and longer lasting than other brands. She then told me a great little story about getting her boyfriend, who works in an automotive shop, to let her paint one of his nails so she could test the polish's staying power under "high-stress conditions," and that it had lasted a week! She didn't try to convince me to buy it. She was simply sharing her positive experience with it. I found this a very attractive introduction to a new product.

These same elements of awareness work well when inviting people to consider the possibility of approaching an issue more strategically. If they feel positive about you, if you personally endorse it without being dogmatic, and if you provide real-world examples or stories of how this process has been helpful in similar situations, people will be more likely to be interested in and open to your message. Here's how that might sound in a work situation:

David Chen is definitely frustrated. This is the third meeting he's sat through with this project team, and they're not getting anywhere. The team leader is a good person, smart and well liked, but she seems unable to get the group beyond everyone's various conflicting opinions about the problem before them. It's even more frustrating because their company—AllTea—is generally pretty fast moving and unbureaucratic. In fact, since being started ten years ago by two ex–Stash employees, AllTea has grown dramatically. That growth has prompted the formation of this cross-functional team. It's been put together to figure out how to create better communication among the company's headquarters and manufacturing facilities and the three—soon to be four—field sales offices. This team has been given two months to offer recommendations to the senior team. They're now in their third week and no closer to agreeing on recommendations—or even how to get to recommendations—than when they started.

Suddenly David remembers the approach he's been using with his own team—he's a VP of New Products—from the book Being Strategic *and decides to offer it to the group. "Hey, guys," he says at the next lull in the conversation, "I want to offer an idea. There's something I've been using with my team lately that's really working well. You all know we were really stuck on the development of the* chai *product last fall, and we used this approach to unblock ourselves and figure out where we needed to go with it."*

The other members of the team turn toward him,

interested—they're all aware that the chai *launched well, with excellent initial sales results. "Please," says Joan, the team leader, "anything." She says it with exaggerated desperation, but David knows she's only half joking. Everybody smiles or nods, murmuring agreement.*

"OK, then," David continues. "It's this process where you define the challenge—and we have ours pretty well defined, I think—then you work together to make sure you have all the relevant information about the situation. After that, you define what success would look like—where you'd want to end up if you met the challenge. Then you try to be really objective about what's in the way—the obstacles—and you create strategies and tactics that will take you from where you are to where you want to go."

Most people are nodding speculatively, but Dominic is frowning. "Sounds like a lot of work just to come up with some recommendations," he says.

David shrugs. "Yeah, I thought that, too. I mean, it's not like we hadn't created new products before! But we were just getting nowhere, and this approach let us step back, get clear about what we were trying to accomplish, then move toward it."

Joan speaks up. "Look, I'm for it. It sounds good to me, and 'getting nowhere' certainly sums up our progress to date. C'mon, Dom, what do you say?"

Dominic looks at David, at Joan, around the table, and then shrugs. "What the hell," he says, looking down. "Sure."

Everybody turns back to David, and Joan says, "All right, David, so how do we do this?"

David has done a good job on the Awareness step; everyone now knows there's another way to approach their task. Fortunately, the team seems to feel pretty positively about David and he presented the process in a way (personal without being preachy, and with a real-life success story attached) that helped them understand and accept the possibility of what he was offering.

However, I'm not convinced that any of them (except maybe Joan) have moved on to the Motivation step. So, let's talk about that step and then see how David can take them through it.

MOTIVATION

In my experience, people are motivated to do something new when they truly feel that it will be personally helpful to them and that it will work better for them than what they're doing now. Feeling that something will be personally helpful to you is very different from thinking you "should" do something.

For instance, up until about six years ago, I knew that I "should" exercise. I was informed about all the benefits, and I was well aware that it was increasingly important to my health as I aged. I just didn't connect with it personally. The benefits were very abstract to me. Then, just after I turned fifty, my siblings and I went to celebrate my mom's eightieth birthday. Two things happened. I saw how frail and weak my mom was—this was a woman who had never exercised since she stopped chasing around after us as little kids—and I saw how wonderful my sister looked. She's only a few years older than I am, and she had recently lost quite a bit of weight through exercise and eating healthier. The contrast between her renewed vitality and beauty and our mom's increasing ill health finally made it real for me: Without exercise: this. With exercise: that. Click: I got it.

So, how can you help people have that "click" about being strategic? I've noticed that people tend to be motivated to change when they're offered—as I was—a clear example of the *personal* rewards of behaving differently and a clear example of the *personal* "anti-rewards" (the risks, hazards, or difficulties) of continuing to behave in the same ways. It doesn't always work, but it seems to work better than anything else.

Let's see how David does this:

"Well," David says, looking at Dom, "let me just sketch it out first, so you'll know what you're in for, and then we can see if we really want to do this."

Everyone looks expectant, except Dom, who's still looking at his notes.

"So," David continues, "here's what you can expect from this process. If we take the next meeting to clearly assess the current reality—the good news and bad news—of communication between the field and home, we could use the second meeting to decide what we'd want communication to be like, our definition of success. Then, the third meeting we could agree on important obstacles to achieving that success. In the fourth meeting we could come up with our recommendations, based on where we're starting from, where we want to go, and what's in the way. And in the fifth meeting we could hone the recs—having had a week to reflect on what we came up

with—and prepare to present them to the senior team." He turns to Joan. "We do have five meetings left, right?"

"Six, actually," she replies, "but that's good—it gives us a cushion." Joan is clearly on board with this idea and ready to roll.

David smiles. "OK, but hold on a minute. Not to play devil's advocate for my own idea, here—but if we did this it would mean committing to a pretty complete process, and I want to make sure everybody thinks it's a good idea. So, what are our alternatives?"

Sharita says, "None that I can see," and most others on the team nod.

Dom looks up and says, clearly frustrated, "Look, we all know that the only thing that's wrong between field and home is that the field offices want to know every little thing that's happening and that's not realistic."

Elinor and Antwan, both of whom work in field offices, start to respond at once:

"Come on, Dom, that's not—"

"Dom, just because you've never—"

"Hold up, you guys," Joan says, stopping their protestations. She turns to Dom. "Look, I'm sorry, but I think it's more complex than that. I for one don't want to spend the next six weeks arguing, and this process David's proposing seems like a useful alternative. Unless, of course, you'd like to go to your boss at the end of the two months and tell him we weren't able to come up with recommendations."

At this, Dom looks suddenly reflective. His boss, the head of Production, is a no-nonsense manager who would definitely not be pleased to hear that his guy had been an obstruction to the team's success. Dom shakes his head, and his mouth quirks. "Well," he says, "if you're going to pull out the big guns . . ." Everybody laughs. "All right," he says. "I'm in. Let's try it."

Dom was clearly motivated by the idea of his personal anti-rewards! Most of the rest of the team seem to have connected with David's description of how the process could get them where they need to go over the next five or six meetings: the personal benefit to them. It looks like they're in a pretty good place to start the process.

Try It Out

It's time to try this out in your own life. I want you to be successful on your first run, so I suggest you pick a situation where using the process of being strategic would be FIT—that is, where you think it's realistic given the group, your relationship to it, and the challenge before you; where using the process would really help; and where you have time to go through the process.

✓ **SELECT A SITUATION:** With "FIT" in mind, select and note below a group challenge you're involved with (this could be at work, in a charitable group, in a school or church committee, etc.) where you'd like to invite the rest of the team into the strategic process:

✓ **AWARENESS:** Note below how you could present the idea of the process to the group so as to personally endorse it without being dogmatic, and including an example or story that will help them "see" it (consider using an example of how you've used the process in your own life):

✓ POSITIVE MOTIVATION: How could you explain the potential personal and group rewards of using the process in this situation—or what questions could you ask to elicit those benefits from the other team members?

✓ NEGATIVE MOTIVATION: Conversely, how could you explain the potential personal and group risks, hazards, or difficulties of not using the process in this situation? Or, even better, what questions could you ask to elicit those anti-rewards from your fellow team members?

All right, then . . . you're ready to invite them into the process. Just to encourage you to actually do this, I invite you to note below how it worked. Did the group agree to go through the process with you? If not, what could you do differently next time a FIT situation comes up for being strategic?

NOW THEY'RE ALL LOOKING AT YOU . . .

. . . with expectant faces. Never fear: I'll take the next three chapters to prepare you to support your team or group through the process. Onward and upward!

In Real Life:

Start by trying the "awareness and motivation" approach in smaller ways, just to get the feel for it. For example, you might want to apply it in talking with your kids (for smaller kids, perhaps introducing new foods; for older kids, perhaps encouraging them to try new activities) or in coaching employees to try new approaches or skills. Think about how you can first make the person aware of the possibility of behaving differently—without being dogmatic, and using personal examples—then think about how you can help him or her see the personal benefit of doing so.

TWELVE

Crafting a Strategic Vision

In the little museum at the entrance to Criccieth Castle, there's a reproduction of a drawing from the time of the castle's building. It shows Llewellyn Fawr standing with some of his nobles, engaged in conversation. The drawing is a bit cartoony—this was before the rediscovery of perspective in Western art—but the intent is clear: Llewellyn is mixing it up with his guys, not sitting apart on a throne telling them what to do.

Generally, when we think of kings and princes and their relationship to their subjects, our mental model tends toward the Norman: big thrones, lots of ceremony and intermediaries. The Welsh were more collegial and familial. Their princes were their most important people, certainly, but that didn't mean you couldn't disagree, question, or joke. And a Welsh prince would be much more likely to share a cup of mead and take an interest in your dogs or your children than to issue decrees and fiats.

And, though simple, the drawing is evocative. You can almost hear these fierce Welshmen speaking over one another, making their points with great passion as they gesticulate and look to heaven.

So I can only assume that, among his other gifts, Llewellyn must have been great at helping guide the conversation, at getting his people to address the key issues and come to some resolution. And that's what we'll look at in this chapter. Now that you've gotten a group aware of this process and motivated to move through it, how, exactly, do you make that happen?

WHAT'S DIFFERENT, WHAT'S THE SAME?

Here's the good news: the basic mind-set and skills of being strategic remain the same, whether you're addressing an issue by yourself or with a group. You'll be moving through the process in conversation with others, not in the privacy of your own head, but the core elements will still be to define your challenge, get clear about the current reality, envision the future you want to create for yourselves, look honestly at "what's in the way," and craft the strategic and tactical path to get you there.

So, this chapter consists of what I've learned over the past twenty years of helping teams and organizations think and act in these ways. It's a collection of time-tested tips and approaches for applying the art of being strategic in a group setting. I've found all of them useful. Take what you believe will work well for you and your group.

FIRST, A CAUTION ABOUT WHERE AND WHEN

Before I dive into the substance of how to do this, I'd like to offer some advice about the importance of environment and timing. I've found, over the years, that it's important to create a dedicated time and place for the initial vision and strategy session. As you know, I'm completely committed to the belief that being strategic is an approach to living the life you want and that it can—and should—be wired into your day-to-day routine. But especially when you're starting out, and especially with a group, it's important to give the mind-set and the process of being strategic a protected space to grow and flourish. It's kind of like starting a plant in a greenhouse!

Generally, I encourage clients to take a couple of days and go off-site to complete this process. That seems to yield the best results. People truly put aside their daily work and come together as a group. It makes it much easier to Fair Witness and to pull back the camera.

If that's simply not possible, you can do it like Alicia at greenbambino.com or David Chen at AllTea did and create a series of dedicated meetings. If that's your approach, I recommend you take big chunks of time—say four half days or six two- to three-hour sessions—so that you can really get traction in each meeting and get a good amount of work done. When you do it this way, it's important (and more challenging!) to make clear agreements with people about being fully engaged in the meetings and being present for all of them. It's difficult, as you might imagine, to miss part of this process and then jump back in.

OK, then—on to the substance. . . .

DEFINE THE CHALLENGE

Shifting the Group's Focus

As you may remember from chapter 2, the easiest way to get clear about the challenge facing you is to ask a series of three questions. (If that fact has slipped your mind, consider the following a friendly review. Of course, you should also feel free to go back and reread the chapter.)

DEFINING THE CHALLENGE

Ask: What isn't working?

Ask: How can we (or I) ... ?

Ask: Would this feel like success?

By approaching the challenge in this way, you can avoid leaping into trying to solve a problem before you're clear on what it is. When you are working with a group to define the challenge, it's even more important to rein in the impulse to leap to solutions before the problem is clearly defined. In the second chapter I showed you a situation where two people started wrangling about opposing solutions. When you're dealing with a group, the opportunities for wrangling multiply geometrically. That's fairly easy to avoid if you have a chance to ask the "defining the challenge" questions before the solutions start flying around—but that rarely happens. Generally, by the time you have a meeting about something that needs to be fixed or a new challenge to be addressed, people are already in full-blown solution mode. So for the most part, when you do this step with a group, you'll be turning people's attention away from their focus on explaining and defending their already-beloved personal solutions. It's kind of like stopping a team of galloping horses. So, here's an approach that's worked well for me over the years in this delicate situation. As soon as I realize that we're arguing solutions without having defined the challenge, I ask the group's permission to share an idea. Then, when they say yes (they're generally so surprised that I didn't just start lobbying for my own solution that they almost always say yes), I say something like, "I'm not sure we're all trying to solve the same problem. What do we think the problem is?"

Most often, somebody will state his or her version of what the problem is in a kind of isn't-this-obvious tone of voice and at least a couple of other people in the room will look surprised and disagree. Before they can start a new argument—about what the problem is—I break in and say, "How about if we all just say what we think is the problem and look for overlaps?" You may have to repeat some version of the "and look for overlaps" phrase a few times. People's impulse toward I'm-right-and-you're-not can be strong. But if you can get the group focused on the task of creating a shared picture of what's not working or what needs to be addressed or accomplished (the challenge), you will have gone most of the way toward shifting their attention.

Then, once the issue is fairly clear, you can just say, "So, what's a good way to state what we're trying to solve for here? As in: "How can we . . . ?" Leave the sentence hanging, and encourage people to complete it by your tone of voice or facial expression or even an inviting hand gesture. Much more often than not, somebody will finish the sentence and the group will then tweak it till it sounds right to everyone. (In the rare case where no one else speaks up, you can take a crack at finishing the sentence yourself, just to get the group started.)

When the group has agreed on the "How can we . . ." question, you can simply ask them the third "defining the challenge" question as it is: "If we found the answer to that, would it feel like success?" And then you can help the group revise the "How can we . . ." question if needed. (If you feel this particular group needs more explanation or context, you might say something like, "Let's make sure we're on the right track here; if we found the answer . . . ," and then complete the third question.)

Try It Out

I'd like you to select a situation that's real for your group or team, one about which you'd really like to be thinking more strategically and that you're reasonably sure the group will accept your help in addressing. Then we'll work through it together in this chapter to prepare you to approach the issue strategically with your teammates. (Please note: you're perfectly welcome to use the situation you selected in the last chapter for your "awareness and motivation" practice.)

✓ Select a problem, a challenge, or an area your team or group needs to explore (it's OK to choose one where the solution wars have already begun), and jot down a few words to describe it. Pick one that you feel will be reasonably straightforward to solve. You don't want your first attempt at group vision and strategy to be so difficult a challenge (world peace, the problem of lost socks) that you're doomed to failure.

_____

_____

_____

_____

_____

_____

✓ **ASK: WHAT ISN'T WORKING?:** Knowing your group and referring to the suggestions above, how might you focus your group away from premature solutions and toward the challenge or problem itself?

_____

_____

_____

_____

_____

_____

✓ **ASK: HOW CAN WE (OR I) ... ?:** Again, knowing your group, and using the approach I've suggested to whatever extent it seems useful, how will you invite them into framing the "How can we ..." question?

_____

_____

_____

_____

_____

_____

_____

✓ **ASK: WOULD THIS FEEL LIKE SUCCESS?:** How will you encourage the group to check their "How can we ..." question to see if answering it would feel like success?

_____

_____

_____

_____

_____

_____

_____

A BIGGER CHALLENGE: PURPOSE

If you simply get the group turned away from the solution debate and toward defining the problem, you will have done them a great service. Before we go on, though, I want to discuss an even more helpful use of this part of the process.

Over the years, as I've supported groups through this process of vision and strategy, I noticed that some groups would gravitate to a much deeper level of challenge. Rather than simply focusing on "How can we assure that we have the lowest error rate in our industry?" or "How can we add field offices and still maintain our culture?" they wanted to focus on "How can we fulfill our purpose as an organization?"

And over time, I came to realize that when I was engaged in vision and strategy with a senior team that wanted to focus on the future of the whole organization, there was an added step. In order to answer the preceding question—how to *fulfill* the purpose of the organization—we needed to first get clear about what *was* the purpose of the organization!

I call this purpose *mission*, as in: "What is your mission as an organization? In other words, why does the organization exist?" Another way of asking this question is: "If your organization didn't exist, what would not happen in the world, or what would happen less well?"

Over the years, some of the client companies with which we've worked have come to answer this question of mission in really compelling and unique ways. For example:

Union Square Hospitality Group: *We enrich and inspire others through hospitality and excellence.*

WICT (Women in Cable Telecommunications): *We develop women leaders who transform our industry.*

AxoGen, Inc: *We return quality of life to patients by creating and delivering superior peripheral nerve solutions.*

Concord Records: *We are a creative and innovative force in the music world, committed to enriching people's lives by delivering music of timeless appeal.*

A clear, simple, and focused statement of mission, like the ones here, becomes a powerful starting point for thinking strategically about a company's future. Here's how the remaining elements of the strategic process for a whole company flow out from mission:

Mission: why we exist, our unique purpose as an organization.

Vision: what we would look like if we were more fully achieving that purpose: our hoped-for future as a company, fulfilling our mission

Obstacles: what might make it difficult for us to be the company we envision, achieving our purpose

Strategies: core directional choices toward becoming the company we envision

Tactics: specific actions that will best implement those strategies

As you can see, the elements of the process don't change; they're just reoriented toward the bright North Star of mission. And like the North Star, one of the great things about a well-crafted mission statement is that it's permanent. If you craft it to represent the core purpose of the organization, it won't be limited by markets or technology; it will be targeted to some essential human need, and you can keep moving toward it for the life of the organization. Look at the four examples I've given earlier: it's unlikely that any of them will be obsolete in ten years, or even twenty. With an "evergreen" mission statement like this, you can keep repositioning your vision and strategies over the years to continue moving in the direction of fulfilling your mission.

CLARIFY WHAT IS

On to Current Reality

Whether the challenge you're working on is something rather modest,—say, "How can we ensure our after-school program stays fun, safe, and cost-effective?"—or more world changing, like, "How can we build mutual respect and understanding between the next generation of Muslims and Jews?" the next step, just as when you're thinking strategically on your own, is to encourage your group to assess the "what is" relative to your challenge.

This is a good point, if you haven't already done so, to walk the group through the whole process (remember awareness and motivation?) in a way that will gain their buy-in. Understanding the process will also help to keep them from leaping into problem-solving mode too soon.

Doing this step thoroughly and thoughtfully will give the whole group a chance to get grounded in the actual facts of the situation—to get a good idea of the important factors affecting the challenge.

Your skills, honed during the first half of the book—of Fair Witnessing, pulling back the camera, and sorting for impact—are going to come in really handy here, and you can support the group by explaining to them these concepts (first introduced in depth in chapter 3) and reminding people of them when it seems appropriate. (I get a big kick out of hearing people I've worked with over the years say, "Hey, let's pull back the camera here; we're getting down in the details," or, "Are we Fair Witnessing, or just seeing what we want to see?" Then I know these approaches have lodged themselves firmly into their way of thinking about important situations.)

I want to build on your skills of pulling back the camera and Fair Witnessing by offering you two frameworks for this step—two ways to organize your group's conversation about "what is." These are simply guidance systems for helping to assure that you look at the most relevant parts of the current reality when working with a group.

The Beauty of SWOT

This framework has been around for a long time and lends itself wonderfully to thinking strategically, if used correctly. Most people in business have heard of or done a "SWOT analysis" (*SWOT* is an acronym for Strengths, Weaknesses, Opportunities, and Threats), but it's often conducted in a way that's not very helpful. First, because people tend to do SWOT in a kind of general, let's-put-everything-in-here kind of way, without sorting for impact, and second, because they misunderstand the best use of the "Opportunities" section.

Let me first explain the SWOT as it applies to the process of vision and strategy with a group, so you can start to understand how to avoid these difficulties.

STRENGTHS: In this section, you focus on the strengths of the group relative to the challenge. So, for instance, let's say your challenge is one of those I mentioned at the beginning of this section: you're part of a parent-teacher task force focused on "How can we ensure our after-school program stays fun, safe, and cost-effective?" Some relevant strengths might be "the person in charge of the after-school budget has great financial skills" or "the kids really like the program."

WEAKNESSES: In this section, as you might suspect, you focus on the weaknesses or deficits of the group relative to the challenge. In this situation, relevant weaknesses might be "we've been kind of lax about emergency procedures" or "we're not clear about what we want the program to provide."

OPPORTUNITIES: This is where traditional SWOT analysis gets a bit fuzzy. I've noticed that many people use this section to focus on opportunities in the sense of "possible things we could do going forward." For our purposes at this point in the process, this isn't very useful, as it takes the group's focus off the present and moves it toward the future. I suggest you use this section to focus on opportunities in the sense of "circumstances around us that support our success." That way, you're still exploring current reality. In this version of a SWOT, opportunities are, in effect, strengths *external* to the group that are relevant to the challenge—that is, outside situations that can serve you. So, for instance, in the after-school challenge, some opportunities might be "lots of other schools have figured out how to do this well and their learning is available to us" or "the whole school community is supportive of our success."

THREATS: This section is the negative analogue of opportunities: circumstances around you that could impede your success. In other words, as opportunities are strengths external to the group, threats are weaknesses external to the group. For instance, "the school isn't in a very safe neighborhood" or "there are likely to be more budget cuts next year."

In fact, if you turn back to pp. 53 and 54, you'll notice that the SWOT framework is basically identical to the approach I suggested for assessing your personal "what is": helpful and unhelpful stuff within you and helpful and unhelpful stuff around you, relative to your challenge. Whether you're doing this alone or with a group, that's most of what you need to know.

Making It Visible

One other suggestion before I go on to the second "framework." I always find it helpful to have somebody write the SWOT elements down where everyone can see them as you're talking through them: on a flip chart, for instance, or a whiteboard. It seems to work well to have four columns, one for each "letter." I've found when it's all laid out visually like this for people, it's easier for them to Fair Witness and to pull back the camera. Something about putting words on a page, publicly, makes it easier to be objective. (That's one of the reasons I encouraged you to write down your individual "what is" assessment in earlier chapters.) And then, when you're done, it's great to have it up there as a map of the present that everyone can refer to as you begin to envision your hoped-for future.

Leading Up to What Is

I want to share one more technique that can support you in assessing current reality with a group. It's called oral history. Often, a group's history is an important part of where they are today and not knowing that history can make it harder to envision a realistic future. Here's a simple example. Let's say that, five years ago, the after-school program school was canceled for almost a year because a child fell from a jungle gym and was seriously hurt. It was a difficult circumstance, with parents very divided over whether the young teacher in charge of the program that day had been negligent. Let's further say that there are three people on the current task force who were around when that happened and six people who weren't. The new people will be missing a critical piece of the current reality, because they won't know about the impact this event has had on the school community and why longtime parents are so particularly concerned about safety. By talking the team through an oral history of the situation (or of the department or company, if you're doing this process at work) you can bring those critical facts to light and factor them into the group's strategic thinking.

I've found this approach is especially helpful where a group contains both "tribal elders"—that is, people who have been around this group or issue for a while and know the history—and "newbies." In such situations, it serves to get everyone on the same page. The oral history approach is also helpful if there have been struggles or difficulties within the group in the past: talking through the history then tends to be both cathartic and informative.

A few months ago, I did just this part of the Being Strategic process for a media client—a cable network with a staff of about eighty people—and they found it extremely valuable for all these reasons. There were people in the group who'd been there since the network began ten years before, one woman who had just started working there that day, and everything in between! And during those ten years, they'd been through changes in ownership, ratings failure and success, one particularly poor president, and some financial skulduggery. After we were done and were taking a break, one of the newer people came up to me and said, "Now I feel like I really know why things are the way they are here. It will help me navigate better."

I noticed that the information they shared helped them to understand more clearly what they needed to let go of, as a group, and the historical strengths they could rely on more as they moved into the future. They've since gone on to create and move toward a clearer vision for their future, taking better advantage of their historical strengths and avoiding past pitfalls.

If you think your group could benefit from adding an oral history to your "what is" assessment, here's an approach for doing it:

1. Explain to everyone the process and why you think it will be useful (awareness and motivation!).
2. Starting with the year the group began or the issue first surfaced, encourage the tribal elders to share the key elements of the history: the people, events, and perceptions—both internal and external—that were most important to the group's (or the issue's) evolution.
3. It's most useful to go year by year; then you can help the group move along by saying things like, "Is that about it for 2002? What about 2003?"
4. Invite people into the process as they come on board. For instance, you can say, "So, who joined the group in 2004? Sally. So, what was happening when you showed up? People, events, perceptions."
5. I've found it most helpful to "scribe" the history on flip charts as people are talking through it. I generally use one flip chart page per year and three different marker colors—one each for people, events, and perceptions. Don't worry about getting it all down. It's useful simply to capture the key ideas as people speak.
6. At the end of the process, I most often ask people to review what's been written and then note one or two things they want to leave behind (e.g., aspects of their history that were counterproductive or that no longer serve them) and one or two things they want to bring forward (e.g., things they've learned, positive elements of their culture, or approaches that will still be helpful). This helps ensure that the group internalizes the lessons of their own past and brings the best of the past into the future.

Try It Out

Now, you'll decide how you might incorporate any or all of the ideas I've outlined here into doing the "what is" part of the process with your group. Focus on the problem, challenge, or area for exploration you chose earlier in the chapter. You can write it down again below, for easier reference, if you'd like.

_____

_____

_____

_____

_____

_____

_____

_____

_____

✓ **FAIR WITNESSING, PULLING BACK THE CAMERA, SORTING FOR IMPACT:** Given your group, note below which of these (it could be all three) will be most helpful to them in getting an accurate sense of your current reality relative to this challenge, and some ideas for introducing these skills and supporting the group in making use of them.

_____

_____

_____

_____

_____

_____

_____

_____

✓ **SWOT:** If you decide to encourage the group to do a SWOT analysis, how will you explain it to them and what will you do to help make it successful?

_____

_____

_____

_____

_____

_____

_____

_____

✓ **ORAL HISTORY:** Decide whether you believe this exercise will be useful to your group, and—if so—note how you'll introduce and manage the process to get the most benefit from it.

_____

_____

_____

_____

_____

_____

_____

_____

ENVISION WHAT'S THE HOPE

Let the Games Begin!

For most groups, this next step feels like the fun part. The first two parts of the process—defining the challenge and then looking at the current situation—most often feel like discipline to people. It's a focused effort. Thinking about the possibilities can feel a lot looser and more open-ended. In fact, it can pretty easily become like kids let out for recess: a lot of fun and running around. High-energy and positive, but not entirely useful at this point.

The art, when doing this step with a group, is to find the right balance between pure creation and disciplined forward movement. First, it helps to remind people that they're envisioning the future in which they've answered the "How can we . . ." question. This will keep people usefully focused. You might also find the phrase "reasonable aspiration" helpful. In my experience, most people find that a useful boundary for their thinking.

Second, I suggest you use the framework I laid out in chapter 4:

ENVISION THE HOPED-FOR FUTURE

Pick a time frame for success

Imagine yourself in that future

Describe what success looks and feels like

Select the key elements

Just as it does when you're thinking individually, this framework will put some boundaries on the ideation process for your group, without constraining it too much.

It's in the Cards

You can simply lead the group through this framework, in the same way I talked you through it in chapter 4, but I'd also like to offer you another alternative. I call it the Post-it technique, and it's a very fun, high-energy way to complete this step of the Being Strategic process, one that we've used for many years with a wide variety of groups. It has the advantage of giving everyone an equal voice in the process and yielding a vision that is truly shared by everyone who participates.

Try It Out

I'm going to walk you through this technique, so you can lead the process yourself. (NOTE: to conduct the step using this approach, you'll need enough three-by-five Post-it notes for everyone in the group to have five or six of them; a thin-line black marker, like a Sharpie, for each person; and a large, flat wall space to put the Post-its on, once everyone has written on them. I'll let you know, later, at what point in the process to hand them out and how to use them.)

✓ **PICK A TIME FRAME FOR SUCCESS:** Have the group pick a point (a specific date) in the future that will allow you all to have made substantive progress toward addressing your challenge. Encourage the group not to envision too far out: even if you're creating a hoped-for future for your whole organization, it's generally best to pick a date no more than three to five years in the future. Further out than that and it can become a confounded experiment—too many variables.

✓ **IMAGINE YOURSELF INTO THAT FUTURE:** I've found it's helpful to say to the group some version of, "OK, now it's the ___ of ___, ___ [the day, month, and year you've selected]. We've come back together to celebrate the fact that we've successfully addressed our challenge [remind them what it is], and to share with each other what's happening in the future we envisioned."

✓ **DESCRIBE WHAT SUCCESS LOOKS AND FEELS LIKE:** When everyone in the group has let you know they're firmly grounded in the future date (if you're not sure, you can ask, "Are we there? Is it April 17, 2012?"), encourage them first to reflect on what they'd like to share with the group: "What has the group accomplished relative to the challenge? How does it look and feel to be in this successful future? What are others seeing and saying about our group?" I've found that most people like to write down what they're thinking about at this point: encourage the group to take a few minutes to reflect and jot down their vision of the hoped-for future.

✓ **SELECT THE KEY ELEMENTS—INDIVIDUAL:** While people are thinking and writing, pass out the Post-its and pens. Once most people seem finished thinking, you'll give them instructions about how to use the pens and Post-its. I've written out these instructions in some detail for you, almost as a script, because this is the most critical part of the process. Here it is:

> *"Now, I'd like you to extract the headlines from your envisioning of this successful future. Pick the five or six elements that are most important to you, and write one of them on each of your Post-it notes, which we'll then call 'cards'.*
>
> *"Be brief—use a phrase or sentence—and capture the essence of what's most important to you about this part of the future you've envisioned.*
>
> *"We're going to put them up on the wall when you're done, so I'd suggest you use the pen I've just given you to write your cards and print, versus write, in large letters." (You can show a sample at this point, a Post-it you've written on as you've just described.)*
>
> *Make sure everyone is clear about the process. (I'd suggest you keep an eye on the group as they write, to make sure everyone's understood—sometimes people try to put all their ideas on one Post-it or write very small, etc.)*

✓ **SELECT THE KEY ELEMENTS—GROUP:** When everyone is finished writing their cards, have them post the cards on the wall in no particular order. Then have everyone come up and read them. Now you'll look for the patterns, to come up with a common vision. Again, let me walk you through how to do this:

> *Pick one person—you or someone else—to be the "Post-it mover." We've found, over the years, that if more than one person tries to organize the cards, the process quickly unravels into chaos!*

Let people know that the object of this part of the process is to "pattern" everyone's key ideas into four to six "buckets." With their direction, you'll be placing the cards into columns of similar ideas. Remind them not to move the cards themselves, but to let the Post-it mover move them, and add that the only other rule is that if there's a disagreement about where a card goes, the person who wrote it gets to be the tiebreaker.

To give them context, tell them that once you've organized the Post-its into columns of like ideas, you'll work together to name each column with a word or phrase that captures the core meaning of that group of ideas.

Pick one card, put it slightly aside from the other cards, high on the wall (this will be the first card in a column), and ask people to point to or direct you to any similar cards. Continue this process until all the cards have been organized into four to six columns. (NOTE: you may have more columns than that after your first pass, in which case you can ask the group to look for columns that are similar enough to be combined.)

Once the Post-its are organized into columns, work with the group to name the columns, one by one. Remind the group that they're looking for a word or phrase that will convey the essence of this element of their hoped-for future; these column titles will be their memory device for the future they want to create for themselves. (NOTE: people often initially gravitate toward titles that carry little unique meaning, like "Finances" or "People." Remind them that these titles are a chance to capture the uniqueness of their vision. So, depending on the cards in a given column, they might, instead, choose something like "Sustainable Profit" or "Strong and Satisfied Team.")

Often, we notice that clients choose creative titles for their vision elements that reflect their business or that arise from shared experience or knowledge. This makes the elements even more unique and evocative, and we find that these phrases can become a part of the shared language of the group, used as verbal reminders to one another to stay focused on the vision. For example, in my company, Proteus International, one of our vision elements is "Proteus Elixir." This captures for us the idea that when clients deal with us, they will feel as though they've drunk a revitalizing potion that makes them strengthened and illuminated. When we're talking about a client, we'll sometimes ask, "Are they drinking the elixir?" to remind ourselves that the core purpose of anything we do with clients is to support them in becoming clearer, stronger, and more capable.

When the process is complete, you might want to create a copy of the outcome for everyone to have. We generally create laminated cards for our clients with their vision elements. Here are the "vision cards" of two clients whose mission statements I shared earlier. The first group chose more creative titles and added an explanatory phrase, while the second chose more traditional ones. Both have been equally effective for them as "markers" of the future they want to create:

Union Square Hospitality Group

USHG 2012:

Bucks County: *Enjoying the rewards of profitability*

Good Bones: *Structures and systems support our growth*

WAH-full: *Living balanced and satisfying lives*

Home Run King: *Best-in-category—again and again*

Gen Next: *Current and future leaders create our success*

Grand Crew: *Employees who live—and love—the vision*

WICT (Women in Cable Telecommunication)

WICT 2010:

We're nationally known for developing women leaders in our industry

We evolve with cable and its new partners

We're a driving force in women's increasing industry leadership

Our programming is key to women's success in our changing industry

We're streamlined, effective, and growing

Clients are often surprised by the power of having created this vision together as a group; it's their agreed-upon blueprint for their "castle on the hill" and serves as a strong focal point for continuing to think strategically.

FACE WHAT'S IN THE WAY

Designated Fair Witness

In chapter 5, when we first explored in depth the idea of looking fearlessly and objectively at obstacles, I noted that many people have a real resistance to doing this or do it in a way that's not helpful. Either they don't want to look at the obstacles at all, for fear of getting de-motivated and losing their forward momentum, or they over-focus on the obstacles and become convinced that the obstacles are insurmountable. When working with a group, you'll most likely be dealing with both of these reactions simultaneously. When an obstacle is mentioned, some of your teammates will immediately try to avoid or fix it, while others may talk at length about how insurmountable it is or how it's out of your control.

The good news is you can use your Fair Witness skills to help bring everyone on the team back toward the center. Not only can you model a Fair Witness approach to looking at the obstacles—being as accurate and evenhanded as possible in your own assessment—but you can also "Fair Witness" other people's reactions and then "pull back the camera" for the group. For instance, if someone states an obstacle and someone else immediately tries to offer a solution for it, you can simply note what's happening: "It sounds like you're trying to solve that problem right now." And then you can offer a more useful alternative, one that pulls back the camera and reminds people of the bigger picture: "How about if we get all the obstacles on the table before we figure out what to do about them?"

The same approach also works if people veer off in the other direction. If someone starts to make a case that a particular obstacle is insurmountable, you can simply respond, as a Fair Witness, "That one doesn't seem solvable to you." And then, "Let's take a look at all the obstacles; then we can decide whether and how to address them."

Generally speaking, if people have agreed to the process and you point out simply and fairly that they've wandered away from it and suggest—without blame—that they come back, you won't get much resistance. (I'll talk a lot more about how to do this in the next chapter, on facilitation.)

When looking at obstacles with your group, I've found it's helpful to take the same approach I recommended in chapter 5, of looking at both "outside" and "inside" obstacles. In a group situation, that translates into obstacles outside the group (in the rest of the company or organization, in the industry, in the world around you) and obstacles within the group (resource constraints, poor process or systems, lack of communication, low morale, insufficient skill or knowledge, etc.). As with the SWOT, I suggest you write down the obstacles on flip charts or a whiteboard in order to have a visual record that everyone can see.

Sorting for Impact in a Group

When you've written down all the obstacles, one task remains—sorting for impact. In a small group or one with very good communication, you can simply talk through this together and probably come up with a clear point of view about which obstacles are most important. However, with a larger group or one where people are less likely to come to a meeting of the minds through conversation, we've used an approach over the years called weighted voting that works very well. Here's how to do it:

1. Let everyone know you'll be prioritizing the obstacles to get a sense of which ones you all feel are most important. Which obstacles have the highest potential

to get in the way of achieving your vision and therefore require the most attention?

2. Let everyone know they each have four votes to use on "outside" obstacles and four on "inside" obstacles.

3. Within a "side," tell the group they can allocate their votes however they want: for instance, they can put all four inside votes on one obstacle, if they think that's most critical; two votes each on the two most important obstacles; three on one obstacle and one on another; or one each on four different obstacles. And the same goes for the outside obstacle votes. This way, they can use their votes to indicate both the ones they think are most important and *how* important they see these obstacles as being.

4. Have everyone write down their vote allocation, then tally them one of two ways:

   • In a small group, you can simply have the group members come up to the flip chart or board and put hash marks next to an obstacle indicating how many votes they gave it; then you can add the hash marks all up when everyone has voted.

   • In a larger group (ten or more) it seems to work better if you call out an obstacle, have people raise a number of fingers to indicate the number of votes they gave it (zero through four), and then you count fingers and write down the total number of votes next to each obstacle.

5. Generally this process results in three or four ob-

stacles on each side getting the majority of the votes. I suggest you circle those and then write them down separately on a new flip chart page or newly erased whiteboard, so people can refer to these highest-priority obstacles as they create strategies and tactics.

Try It Out

Now, continuing with the group challenge you've chosen for this chapter, you'll think about how to complete this "what's in the way" part of the process.

✓ **SET-UP:** How will you explain this "what's in the way" step to people in a way that will help them see how useful it is? How will you help reduce their tendency to either avoid or over-focus on the obstacles to your vision?

_____

_____

_____

_____

_____

_____

_____

_____

_____

✓ **FAIR WITNESSING, PULLING BACK THE CAMERA:** Given your group, note below some self-talk you can use to support yourself in being the "designated Fair Witness" for the group as they look at the potential obstacles:

_____

_____

_____

_____

_____

_____

_____

_____

✓ **SORTING FOR IMPACT:** Decide which approach you'll suggest for doing this—conversation or weighted voting—and make notes to yourself about how you can assure whichever approach you use is helpful to the group:

_____

_____

_____

_____

_____

_____

_____

_____

If You Skip the Obstacles, Proceed at Your Own Risk

History is littered with the bones of people who failed to accurately assess the obstacles to their vision. From Napoléon's failure to factor in the severity of the Russian winter to the Bush administration's floundering in Iraq, not looking at the obstacles to your hoped-for future is simply not a good idea.

A couple of years ago, I got to experience one cautionary tale about not looking at obstacles turn into a happily-ever-after. A CEO with whom I work had been improving the "process" side of his business as a part of his overall vision for success. For instance, he had asked his chief financial officer to simplify and speed up the expense reimbursement process and financial reporting; he'd agreed with his chief administrative officer on making a variety of systems—from information technology to human resources—smoother and more user-friendly. However, the legal and business affairs function was still not working well. In fact, it was *so* not working well that executives were running up huge bills using outside counsel, because they couldn't get their needs met internally: using internal lawyers was confusing because their roles and capabilities were unclear, and when they did take on a project, it took far too long—deals had been lost and relationships damaged as a result.

For months, the CEO kept encouraging people to use the inside legal staff, exhorting them to be "team players" and to "be frugal." He avoided acknowledging the real obstacle: the general counsel. While an excellent lawyer, he was completely ineffectual as a leader and manager of the legal function.

Finally, the CEO "faced what was in the way." He looked

at the legal function with clear eyes and saw the most critical obstacle to success. He let the GC go (a personally difficult decision, as they had worked together for many years) and brought in a new GC who had the necessary skills. Within six months, the bills for outside counsel had been reduced by 60 percent.

DETERMINE WHAT'S THE PATH: STRATEGY

Start from Zero

The single most useful piece of advice I have to offer about doing this part of the process with a group is *assume there is no clear understanding of strategy*. I know this may sound strange, especially if the group you're working with is senior and experienced. But trust me on this: even if everyone in the group is a CEO, with dozens of years' experience, it won't hurt to start from scratch. What do I mean by this? Two things: (1) offer, and get agreement on, a common definition for being strategic (I invite you to use the one in this book—I've never had a group disagree with it); and (2) provide an example of the difference between strategy and tactics (feel free to use the FDR example in chapter 6—again, I've never worked with a group that didn't find it useful).

Even if people in the group are naturally strategic, bringing the process to everyone's conscious awareness is, I've found, extremely helpful. It assures that everyone's efforts will be focused on crafting clear strategy, not arguing about what strategy is. Once you've done that and gotten everyone on the same page, here's how I'd suggest you proceed.

MAKE THE PROCESS VISIBLE: Post the flip charts you've made that capture the first three elements of the process—"What Is" (SWOT and/or history), "What's the Hope" (your vision elements), and "What's in the Way" (the most important obstacles)—where everyone can see them. Review them aloud, and then note that you're now defining "what's the path"—how to get from "what is" to "the hope." I often make the visual metaphor even clearer by creating, on a flip chart page, a drawing like figure 3 (the point is clearly not the quality of the art!). I say something like,

Figure 3

"X marks the spot—that's where we're starting from. This castle on the hill is our vision of the future. And the obstacles are the steep parts of the mountain, and the trolls hiding in the cracks." Then I draw an arc from the X to the castle and continue, "And now we're going to define our path from where we are to where we want to be by first agreeing on our core directional efforts—our strategies—and then filling in that path [at this point I usually sketch in a few "cobblestones"] with tactics."

Having a visual "anchor" like this seems very helpful to people.

INVITE PEOPLE TO CONVERSE: You might want to start the conversation by saying something like, "So, what's one core directional effort we'll have to make to get to our castle on the hill?" When someone offers an idea, invite others to respond and build on it.

KEEP PULLING BACK THE CAMERA: If someone offers as a strategy something that seems like a tactic (e.g., "we need to talk to IT and find out what it will cost to upgrade the software we're using"), invite everyone to step back. You can do this by saying something like, "Let's pull back the camera. What overall effort is that action a part of?" This will most often result in a useful conversation, one that questions the assumptions often inherent in too-quick focus on tactics. For instance, the group might ultimately create a strategy like "determine optimum software needs and costs to implement our vision."

KEEP IT SIMPLE: Sometimes people create very complex strategy statements because they're trying to stuff all the related tactics into them! For example, a group I once worked with wanted to have as a strategy "create an HR approach that includes performance management, succession planning, good hiring and retention practices, and a revamped HRIS system." (!) I encouraged them to restate it as "create and implement a comprehensive HR approach that fully supports our vision of the future," by noting that defining the appropriate elements of the plan would be part of the tactics for that strategy.

USE FIT: Feasibility, Impact, and Timeliness are even more useful in a group than when thinking on your own. For whatever reason, groups working together in sessions like this have a strong tendency to commit to deeply unrealistic courses of action. Maybe it's a kind of mass amnesia—easy to forget about all your other commitments in a rush of group enthusiasm for the work at hand! Whatever the reason, you can really help by reminding people of the need for strategies to be feasible, impactful, and timely. One important aspect of feasibility is the number of strategies defined. I usually encourage a group to "pick their shots" by selecting the three to five highest-impact, most feasible, most timely strategies. More than that—even if they're really great strategies—and the group is unlikely to be able to follow through effectively.

Try It Out

Use the space below to decide how to complete the strategy part of the "what's the path" step with your group. (Continue to focus on the challenge you've used throughout this chapter.)

✓ **SETUP:** How will you explain strategy (and the difference between strategy and tactics) so as to get everyone's understanding, agreement, and buy-in?

_____

_____

_____

_____

_____

_____

_____

_____

_____

✓ Thinking about your group, its members, and your experience of discussions you've had in the past, how will you help the conversation move forward and stay on a strategic level?

_____

_____

_____

_____

_____

_____

_____

_____

✓ How will you help the group create simple strategies to which they can realistically commit?

_____

_____

_____

_____

_____

_____

Since I shared two of our clients' vision elements earlier in this chapter, I thought you might like to see the strategies they created to achieve them, as well:

Union Square Hospitality Group

Strategy 1: Create and implement a comprehensive approach to continuously growing "generation next"

Strategy 2: Operationalize a focus on profitability that is consistent with our culture

Strategy 3: Build a UHSG that can sustain and polish our core businesses, grow businesses, and create "new uniques" with discipline and brand luster

WICT

Strategy 1: Expand to new constituencies within the industry

Strategy 2: Establish WICT membership as a career-long connection

Strategy 3: Build operational and governance systems that are adaptive and scalable

Strategy 4: Consistently evolve our programming to be relevant, accessible, and impactful

Strategy 5: Establish WICT as a recognized authority on women as leaders

DETERMINE WHAT'S THE PATH: TACTICS

The Home Stretch

Groups are usually pretty good with this part of the process: tactics are where the majority of people feel most comfortable, and having the structure of clear vision and well-crafted strategies within which to operate makes it much, much easier to create good tactics.

However, having a group of people working on tactics—instead of just you—makes it even more important to follow the tactical planning guidelines I laid out in chapter 8:

--- **EXCELLENT TACTICS** ---

Arise from strategy

Are FIT

Define what, who, and when

You can most help your group by keeping these guidelines in mind, being attentive to whether or not they're being followed, and bringing the group back if they stray.

I would particularly encourage you to help the group hold itself accountable to "who and when." It's all too easy, in the flow of conversation, to agree on the "what" and then not make anyone accountable for doing it or forget to set a time for it to be completed. I'd also suggest that you and your group select a single person (or, at most, two) to be responsible for each tactic. When you name a group of people as the "who" for a tactic, it's much more likely that no one will take full responsibility for it and it will fall by the wayside. You can make this easier by letting the group know that the "who" for a tactic doesn't have to complete the whole thing alone—he or she is simply the point person, the one who's taking responsibility for making sure it gets done. "You're Tom Sawyer," I often say to the point person for a given tactic. "Get whoever you can to help you paint the fence!"

Divide and Conquer

If your group is large (more than ten or twelve people), it's often helpful to divide into subteams to develop the tactics. Here's a process for doing that:

1. Suggest that you can make efficient use of your time and take advantage of people's expertise and interest by dividing into smaller groups to work on tactics.
2. Write down each of the strategies and ask people to decide for which one they'd like to develop tactics (encourage them to select the one that interests them most and about which they have the most knowledge or experience). Ask them to make a second choice, in case their first choice isn't available.
3. While people are deciding which group they'd like to join, mentally divide the number of people in the group by the number of strategies—this will be the maximum number of people in a group. (For example, if there are fifteen people and four strategies, each group will have a maximum of four people.)

4. Before asking people which group they want to be in, note that a group will be "closed" as soon as it has the maximum number of people. Write down each person's name beside the strategy he or she selects, closing each group as it becomes filled.

5. Once everyone has chosen a strategy group, remind them of the tactical planning guidelines (tactics arise from strategy; are FIT; include what, who, and when) and provide them a time frame in which to work. Note that if they want to name someone not in their group as the point person for a tactic, they need to get that person's OK.

6. When everyone comes back together, have each group share their tactics. Everyone in the larger group needs to either sign off on each tactic or, if they have any major concerns, suggest revisions or alternatives.

Try It Out

To complete the group challenge you've chosen for this chapter, you'll prepare for this final step of the process.

✓ **SETUP:** Decide how to share the tactical guidelines with your group in a way that will help them understand how to create clear and useful plans.

_____

_____

_____

_____

_____

_____

✓ **WHO AND WHEN:** Given your group, note the best approach for making sure they agree on point people and time lines for each tactic:

_____

_____

_____

_____

_____

_____

✓ **DIVIDE AND CONQUER:** If you decide to split the group up into subteams to do tactical planning, note to yourself how you'll set that up:

_____

_____

_____

_____

_____

_____

Greenbambino

I want to review for you the tactics that Alicia and her Marketing and PR group agreed on in chapter 8—now you'll appreciate what a great job they did creating FIT, strategy-focused tactics with "what, who, and when" clearly defined. Here's their first strategy:

> *Strategy 1: Find out how we're now seen (and what's wanted) re "expertness" by our customers, suppliers, and the press.*

And here are the tactics they devised for that first strategy:

Tactic 1:
What: Draft a questionnaire about current perceptions
  and future needs/desires of our three constituencies
Who: Damian
When: Friday

Tactic 2:
What: Work with team to review and revise questionnaire
Who: Damian
When: Monday's staff meeting

Tactic 3:
What: Draft and present an approach for using the
  questionnaire in an online survey of the customers,
  with some incentive to respond, and phone interviews with key suppliers and press contacts

Who: Ella
When: Monday's staff meeting

Tactic 4:
What: Work with team to create an overall time line for completing the questionnaires, doing the surveying and interviewing, and getting the information organized
Who: Joel
When: Monday's staff meeting

Tactic 5:
What: Create an initial analysis of the information received from the survey and interviews
Who: Joel
When: three weeks after data is collected (per time line in tactic 4)

READY, SET, ALMOST GO

Like our historical friend Llewellyn, you're now well prepared to work with your group to envision and create a "castle" of your own design. Unlike Llewellyn, though, you have one other, very twenty-first-century challenge. . . .

In Real Life:

Start by exercising your Being Strategic skills in lower-risk group situations: for example, deciding where to go on a family vacation, or working with a few colleagues on a small project. You can do each part of the process simply: Agree on the "How can we . . ." through informal discussion; quickly assess the key elements of your current situation; discuss your hoped-for future (what "success" would look like); note any critical obstacles. Then decide on a few core strategies and simple tactics to implement them. This will give you a feeling for completing the process with a group in an easy and natural way.

THIRTEEN

The Art of Facilitation

In this chapter, Llewellyn Fawr isn't such a great example. Even though he was less a divine-right-of-kings and more a let's-ride-off-to-battle-together sort of leader, this was still the thirteenth century and he had enormous power within his realm (for instance, Llewellyn once had a noble hung summarily for being found in his wife Joan's bedroom in a compromising situation, and said wife imprisoned for a year). When it came to getting a group of his nobles to come to a consensus, I suspect his powers of persuasion, combined as they were with the threat of death or exile, were powerful motivators. He didn't really need to be a great facilitator.

You, however, are in a different situation. Even if you are the leader of a group, and even if you now feel confident about your own ability to be strategic, and even if (based on the last chapter) you know how to apply the core tenets of being strategic when working with a group, you still have one more challenge. How do you actually manage the conversation to lead the group to a successful outcome, since, unlike for Llewellyn, the threat of death is not (I hope) available to you?

At this point, you're faced with a choice. You can hire it done—that is, find a skillful third-party facilitator with whom you can share the process and who can guide you and your folks through it—or you can learn to do it yourself. On the one hand, the benefits of getting someone else to do it are (1) there are people who do this for a living and are very good at it, and (2) it allows you to be a full participant in the discussion, rather than toggling back and forth between the facilitator role and the leader role. On the other hand, the benefits of doing it yourself are (1) it gives you a chance to get good at a valuable skill set (the skills of facilitation needed to move a group through this process will help you move any group through any process), and (2) you can use it to help your team be strategic at any time, rather than waiting for an "offsite" with an outside facilitator.

Of course, you can also choose to do both—you may want to pull in a professional facilitator for bigger, more critical conversations (for instance, facilitating your company's yearly vision and strategy session) and facilitate ongoing strategic conversations yourself.

At this point, you may be thinking you don't need these skills. It might feel like something you don't want to learn ("Forget it . . . I'm hiring somebody!") or something you already know how to do ("Facilitator, schmacilitator, I can do this just fine, thanks"). In either case, I invite you to turn to the next chapter.

However, if you want to learn some skills for facilitating a group process more effectively, given the benefits, read on. . . .

WHAT IS A FACILITATOR?

Let's start with a definition. The Merriam-Webster dictionary defines "facilitate" in three simple words: "to make easier." When you're acting as facilitator for a group, your goal is to make it easier for all its members to give of their enthusiasm and expertise, to work effectively together, and to achieve excellent results. Good facilitators:

- listen and encourage listening
- push for depth of discussion on important issues
- keep the focus on the subject at hand
- encourage teamwide participation
- help prioritize issues
- ask "reality check" questions
- help resolve and/or manage differences
- push for closure when appropriate
- support the group to achieve its goals

This is a fairly tall order. However, being a good facilitator is made dramatically easier if you have three things: a clear understanding of the process you've decided to use (in this case, the process of being strategic, so you're set there), the mind-set of a facilitator, and the skills of a facilitator. Let's talk just a bit about mind-set, and then we'll spend the rest of this chapter on the skills.

SETTING YOUR MIND TO FACILITATION

What is "the mind-set of a facilitator"? It's our shorthand for a set of demonstrated beliefs that my colleagues and I have found—both in our work with clients and among ourselves—makes for successful group facilitation.

 The mind-set of a facilitator: to advocate for fairness, honesty, and consensus rather than for a particular person, point of view, or solution

Many a meeting has run off the rails because the person trying to facilitate wasn't able to maintain the open-mindedness and neutrality necessary for getting a group's best thinking and began to try to "run" the meeting (e.g., impose his or her point of view). Of course, when you're facilitating you'll often have your own opinions about the issue under discussion (and I'll talk later about how to contribute your point of view without sabotaging the facilitator's role). However, your success as a facilitator is dependent on your being able to put aside your own beliefs and preconceptions to the extent that you can function as an advocate for fairness, honesty, and consensus.

FAIR WITNESSING YET AGAIN

This may all be starting to sound very familiar to you. It's really just another opportunity to practice your Fair Witness skills. Good facilitation rests on being objective and impartial—on being a Fair Witness. And, as you may recall

213

from chapter 5 and subsequent discussions, *managing your self-talk* is key to Fair Witnessing. It's true here, too. Let me give you some examples. Let's say someone was facilitating a meeting and as she worked with the group, she was thinking things like, *Only a few people here have useful opinions,* or, *I already know what we should do, but I have to make it look like I'm involving people in this decision.* How might that translate into her work with the group?

I suspect that kind of self-talk might lead her to encourage some people to talk and to discourage others, to support some points of view and dismiss or minimize others, to subtly or overtly push for a specific conclusion. Both the process and the outcomes would be negatively impacted by her self-talk.

So, how could she manage her self-talk in order to maintain the mind-set of a facilitator and therefore be more useful to the group in that role? If she used the Recognize, Record, Revise, Repeat model I talked about in chapter 5, she'd first bring to her conscious awareness what she was saying to herself (for instance, *only a few people here have useful opinions*). Then she'd write it down. Then she'd revise it to be more in line with *being an advocate for fairness, honesty, and consensus* (the facilitator's mind-set) and still be believable by her. Perhaps she'd change it to *we need to consider everyone's ideas—there might be hidden gems,* or *if I don't include all the participants, it's unlikely we'll have buy-in.* You get the idea. Then, as she was facilitating, whenever she noticed herself drifting toward advocating for a particular person, point of view, or solution, she'd repeat her revised, impartial self-talk.

Try It: Managing Your Self-talk

Now you'll have a chance to do the same thing: create a good mental foundation for yourself as a facilitator.

✓ Think about yourself in the role of facilitating the vision and strategy process with a group. It's best to get as close as possible to reality: imagine yourself in that role with a team or group you would actually like to invite into this process with you. What self-talk might you be prone to have that would make it difficult for you to remain in the mind-set of a facilitator? Choose a specific unhelpful self-talk statement you might find yourself thinking in this situation and record it below:

✓ Write revised self-talk that you could use in this situation: self-talk that you would believe and that would support you in maintaining the mind-set of a facilitator:

✓ Finally, note a few ideas for "repeating"—for making this rethought self-talk a new mental habit as you're facilitating:

FACILITATOR SKILLS

Now that you can use your knowledge of managing self-talk to approach the role of facilitator with—as my mother used to say—good mental hygiene, let's go on to how you actually do the job. In my experience, the vast majority of what constitutes good facilitation requires these three simple (not easy, but simple) skills:

--- **FACILITATOR SKILLS** ---

Clarify

Protect

Keep on Track

CLARIFY: This skill is a combination of listening and providing feedback, and it allows you to push for depth, summarize, resolve confusion, and reduce miscommunication.

Using this skill helps you make sure everyone understands one another as clearly and fully as possible, and it also helps you point out to the group where they're stuck or—conversely—when they've come to a conclusion. Clarifying avoids wasting time and energy on needless misunderstanding or circular conversations. (These go round and round, full of repetition, becoming increasingly tangled and confused. Sound like meetings you've been in?)

PROTECT: This skill, also based on feedback, encourages full participation by making sure people have the chance to speak and to be heard. It's the "fairness" part of the facilitator mind-set. You use this skill to assure the group benefits from everyone's wisdom and experience and also to assure concerns and disagreements are aired and resolved.

By using this skill, you keep people from steamrolling others—dismissing or drowning out their opinions—and you do it in a way that's fair and respectful not only to the "steamrollees" but to those doing the steamrolling as well.

KEEP ON TRACK: This skill requires, once again, a good grounding in listening and giving feedback. It also requires a full understanding of the process you're using (in this case, the process of being strategic) to help the team maintain focus, prioritize issues, check proposals against reality, and get closure.

Used together, these three skills balance high-quality, fully engaged group process with forward movement and excellent results.

Clearly, being a reasonably skilled listener and giver of feedback is key to being a good facilitator. If you're fluent in these skills, lucky you! However, if you're not, I strongly suggest you put some time into learning them. At the risk of seeming wildly self-referential, I might suggest that you read chapters 1 and 7 in another book I've written called *Growing Great Employees;* those chapters will provide you with a good practical grounding in listening and giving feedback.

Before Going on to Skills

We're about to dig into these skills of clarifying, protecting, and keeping on track, but before we do, I want go back to something I mentioned earlier: that it's possible to facilitate and still contribute to a meeting. The key is letting people know which role you're playing at any given moment. For instance, during a discussion you're facilitating, when you believe you have something of value to add as a participant, you might say, "I'd like to take off my facilitator hat for a minute here, if that's OK with everyone: I have a comment to make from my own perspective." Once you've gotten the group's OK, say what you have to say, and then note that you're returning to the facilitator's role. By doing this, you can maintain the integrity of the facilitator's role and still participate in the discussion.

Now, on to skills. . . .

Clarify

I imagine you've experienced one of the most common problems in meetings: the miscommunication and frustration that arise when people don't understand one another and *think they do*. It's especially likely when people are passionate about their points of view and so are more focused on what they're saying than on listening carefully to others. Part of your job as a facilitator is to be on the lookout for signs of this sort of confusion or misunderstanding—and then surface and resolve it. That's the essence of the Clarify skill.

CLARIFY
- notice lack of clarity
- say what you see/ask for clarification
- check for clarity

NOTICE LACK OF CLARITY: Children, I've often observed, are generally quite good at knowing—and letting you know—when they don't understand something. They'll ask, "Why?" or, "What do you mean?" or, "How does that work?" without hesitation or embarrassment. Unfortunately, as we grow older, we learn to hide our lack of clarity for fear of looking stupid or unprepared. And eventually, most of us actually lose much of our power to discern our own level of understanding or lack thereof. As a facilitator, you need to reverse this process, to re-hone your sensitivity to any lack of clarity in yourself or others and overcome your own resistance to acknowledging it.

Here are three places to look for a lack of clarity and some clues about how to recognize it when you see it:

- **In the speaker:** Is he or she using clichés or jargon that could mean many things? Is he or she hesitating, starting sentences over, seeming to repeat what's already been said?
- **In the group:** Are people looking glazed or perplexed? Do they seem suddenly uncomfortable in their chairs? Are people making comments that don't seem—from your perspective—to have anything to do with what's been said, or seem to be based on a misunderstanding?
- **In yourself:** To be an effective facilitator, you also need to learn to recognize and acknowledge lack of clarity in yourself. I've found that each person has his or her own internal indicators of not being clear. Your signals may be emotional (you might feel suddenly

panicky, anxious, or frustrated), mental (your mind wanders, you have difficulty making connections between statements, or your self-talk gets negative), or physical (you feel a tightness in shoulders or stomach, or your body feels awkward or heavy). By learning to recognize these signs in yourself, you'll create a sort of personal "lack of clarity" alarm system. Remember, the odds are if you're not clear, others aren't, either—and you can help the whole group by acknowledging your own confusion or lack of understanding.

SAY WHAT YOU SEE/ASK FOR CLARIFICATION: This is where your feedback skills will be put to use. You'll simply summarize whatever lack of clarity you observe or feel and ask the person speaking to clarify in as specific, neutral, and timely a way as possible.

For instance, let's say you notice you're not feeling clear about what's being said. If you respond, "I don't get what you're saying," or, "What do you mean by that?" the speaker has no way of knowing what's unclear or how to say it differently (and may get defensive, as well). Instead you could say something like, "John, I don't know exactly what you mean when you say 'people aren't on board.' Could you give me some examples or go into more detail about that?"

Or let's say, instead, that you notice someone else isn't understanding the speaker. Rather than saying, "Alice, you're not getting what John is saying" (again, not helping John and making Alice feel defensive, to boot), you might say, "Alice, it sounds like you think John is advocating x, but I'm not sure that's the case. John, could you say a little more about your position on x?"

Or you might see that people are saying the same thing but aren't hearing or understanding each other. (I call this situation violent agreement!) In this case, you can simply say something like, "Darla, Sam, I think you're actually expressing very similar ideas. Sam, are you saying *XYZ*? And Darla, is that your point of view, as well?"

Finally, a group may not recognize when they've reached a conclusion, because they're all caught in the momentum of discussion. When that happens, you can say, "It sounds like you're all pretty much in agreement on this point—it seems like the consensus is *ABC*. Is that accurate?"

CHECK FOR CLARITY: Once you've surfaced any lack of clarity or misunderstanding and clarification has been offered, check to make sure everybody (speaker, group, you) is clear before moving on.

You can check first by looking to make sure the "lack of clarity" signals you saw earlier are gone. You can also do verbal checks, using your listening skills; either restate what's been said, to make sure you and others are really clear, or ask a curiosity-based checking question like, "Does anybody need to find out anything else before we go on?"

HOW DOES IT LOOK?
At the end of this chapter, I'll have you choose a situation for facilitating a group through a process and I'll guide you to think how you'll use all three skills and incorporate the mind-set of a facilitator. For now, though, I'd like to provide you with an example, so you can get a sense of how using these skills looks in real life. Let's go back to our friend David, who has convinced

his cross-functional task force at AllTea to try applying the vision and strategy process to their challenge: "How can we create better communication among the company's headquarters and manufacturing facilities and the three—soon to be four—field sales offices?" We'll drop in on them to see how David's using the Clarify skill during the "what is" step.

The CTF, as they've starting calling themselves (for "Communication Task Force"), is getting ready to start their next meeting. Before the meeting, David set up the room with two flip charts, each with two columns: "Strengths|Weaknesses" on one and "Opportunities|Threats" on the other. As everyone arrives and gets settled, he realizes that they've never all formally introduced themselves. They basically just started arguing at the beginning of the first meeting and never stopped. He's not even sure the headquarters people know the field folks' names or jobs, and vice versa.

So he begins the meeting by noting that fact ("Here we've been disagreeing for weeks, and we don't even know which department to blame for being wrong!" he says, getting a laugh) and asking everyone to introduce themselves with their name, their job, and where they work. "I'll start," he says. "I'm David, and I'm VP of New Products. I work here in Denver at HQ." He looks to his right.

Joan points at herself, eyebrows raised. David nods. "I think you all know me," she says. "I'm Joan, head of PR and Communications, and I also work here in Denver." She turns to David. "And supposedly I'm head of this task force, but boy, am I glad you're doing this and not me." Everybody laughs again.

The man next to Joan says, "I'm Antwan, director of distri-

bution for the Eastern—soon to be Northeastern—Region. I work out of the New Jersey field office. And I'm really glad we're getting this team off the dime!" He gestures to his right, invitingly.

The woman to his right nods, smiling. "Hey, everybody. I'm glad we're doing this—the intros. I definitely don't know all you guys. I'm Elinor, and I'm VP of Sales for the Western Region, working out of the LA office."

The older man sitting on her right says, "You all know me, 'cuz last meeting Joan and David kept picking on me." Everybody smiles, and Joan shakes her head in mock exasperation. "I'm Dom," he continues, "head of Production Systems, working here in Denver."

"They can't pick on you too much, Dom—I'm in HR," the next person says. She looks around the table. "I'm Sharita, director of Field HR, operating out of the Central Region office in Chicago."

"And I'm Aaron, Comptroller, HQ," says the next person.

"Sadly, we all know you, Aaron," deadpans the last member of the team. Everyone grins. "I'm Luis," he says, "VP of Customer Relations, also here at HQ."

David's happy to see the team's lightheartedness. He hopes it bodes well for the process. He spends a few minutes reviewing the "what is" step of the process, noting both why it's useful and how to do it. He explains the "SWOT" tool as a good way to complete this step and then invites people to begin with strengths that are relevant to their challenge.

"I think we have pretty good communication within each office," Joan begins. "So that's a strength. That means we know how to communicate at least on some levels." David scribes as she talks.

"OK, and I'd say we have the communication infrastructure we need," says Antwan.

David notes a few puzzled looks. "I'm not sure what you mean by that, Antwan," he says. "Could you say a little more?"

"Oh yeah, I just mean we have a good, networked computer system with a pretty robust intranet, our phone system works well, that stuff."

People nod, understanding, and David notes the essence of Antwan's point: "Good communication technology," he writes down. "Is that it?" he asks, and Antwan nods.

Elinor says, "I'm not sure this is a strength—maybe it's an opportunity, actually, or a threat. Or . . . I'm not sure. What's an opportunity, again?"

David answers, "It's an external condition that supports our success."

"Oh, then. It's kind of like—well, I don't know how to say this exactly, but there's the fact that our competitors are actually smaller, for the most part, and don't have field offices. Well, Celestial Seasonings does, but not most of the others. And they aren't having to deal with this kind of stuff, because they're all right there with each other every day. It's like the problems of success. When we were smaller, we didn't have to think about this kind of stuff. . . ."

David notices others starting to shift in their chairs, and he notices his own shoulders getting tight—a sure sign, for him, of confusion. He gently interrupts. "Elinor, wait a second. Are you saying that this lack of communication between field and the home office is a problem most of our competitors don't have?"

"Yes, exactly!" She looks relieved at his clarification.

"All right," he says, "then I think we should put it in the threat column—it's a competitive advantage for them, right?" She nods.

David writes briefly, then turns back to the group. "OK, more strengths?"

Let's turn away while David's on a roll. He did massive amounts of clarifying here. Let me count the ways:

- Having people introduce themselves and what they do is a part of clarifying. Knowing who people are and what they bring to the party is essential to working together well. It helps you understand everyone's frame of reference and take best advantage of their experience and knowledge. David realized it hadn't been done (notice lack of clarity), stated that fact, and invited people to introduce themselves (say what you see and ask for clarity). In this case, he didn't need to check for clarity, but he could have—if someone had looked puzzled when Dom said he was "head of Production Systems," for instance, David could have asked him for a bit of explanation.

- Explaining the process—in this case, David's explanation of the what, why and how of the "what is" step and introducing the SWOT—is part of clarifying, as well. People can work much more effectively when they know what's expected of them, why it's important, and how to do it.

- Writing down the core of people's comments is

clarifying, too. It's a written form of "restating"—the listening skill of summarizing the essence of the speaker's message. It lets the speaker know you've understood and provides a clear record of key points for the group.

- Asking for more explanation from Antwan was pure "clarify." David noticed people's puzzled looks, said he wasn't clear and asked for clarification, and made sure there was clarity by writing down the essence and looking to Antwan for confirmation.
- Untangling Elinor's somewhat rambling comment was also a classic example of clarifying. In this case, David noticed others' signs of confusion and his own "internal warning sign" for confusion, asked for clarification, and checked for clarity by recommending that her point be put under "threats" and getting her OK.

David's doing an excellent job facilitating so far, and I suspect the group is feeling clearer already. Let's go on to the next skill. . . .

Protect

In describing the mind-set of the facilitator, I noted the importance of being an advocate for fairness. That's the essence of this skill: you're *protecting* the right of each group member to contribute to the discussion and to have his or her contributions respected. Here's what it consists of:

PROTECT

- get agreement about behaviors
- notice whether the agreement is honored
- say what you see/ask for what's needed

GET AGREEMENT ABOUT BEHAVIORS: You can't hold people accountable for something they haven't agreed to do, so it's very important that you get agreement with the group up front about how they're going to behave toward one another. In this step, you use the "camera check" element of your feedback skills to let people know exactly what you're asking of them. (NOTE: For a full explanation of "camera check," you may want to read chapter 7 of *Growing Great Employees*. You can also find a brief description at the end of this chapter.)

For example, if you're about to facilitate a brainstorm, you might preface it by saying, "During this part of the process, you'll just be throwing out ideas. In a brainstorm, no one may disagree with anyone else's idea for any reason—we'll have a chance to do that later. If people start discussing or contradicting any of the ideas that are offered, I'll remind them that's not a part of this process. Is that OK with everybody?"

In order to communicate your expectations clearly, in a "camera check" way, you need to know what you want to have happen. For example, in a group discussion where people *can* disagree with one another, how would you describe what's acceptable in terms of behaviors toward others that allow for differences of opinion without putting anybody down? Being clear in your own mind about how people need to interact during a particular process is the best foundation for getting clear agreements with the group.

You can also encourage the group to make their own agreements about how they'll work together. One way to do this: restate the challenge ("How can we . . . ?") and then ask the group, "How do you want to behave toward each other as we work together to address this issue? That is, what road rules do we want to make for our group?"

Then, when people respond, help them frame the "road rules" as behaviorally as possible. For instance, if someone says, "We should be open," you might say, "What would that look like?" And the group might define "open" as "listening to ideas that are new or that you don't agree with" or "taking in feedback or disagreement without defending your point of view."

NOTICE WHETHER THE AGREEMENT IS HONORED: This step requires that you keep the agreement in mind while facilitating the process. You may want to note the essence of the agreements you've made on a flip chart page to post for the group; this will help both you and the group remember and hold yourselves accountable to the agreements you've made.

Independent of the specific "road rules" you've made with the group, though, it's always useful to ask yourself, *Is everyone getting a chance to make a contribution and have it considered fully?* Here are some problems to watch for:

- Are some people's ideas being dismissed before being fully explained (e.g., others saying, "That won't work," or, "We've tried that," or, "You don't understand the situation")?

- Are people defending their own ideas instead of listening to others' ideas?
- Are some people dominating the discussion by monologuing, diverting, or interrupting?

SAY WHAT YOU SEE/ASK FOR WHAT'S NEEDED: As in clarifying, you'll use feedback skills to do this step. You need to state your observations and request the needed change in as specific, neutral, and timely a way as possible.

As soon as you notice, for instance, that someone is interrupting someone else, you can simply say, "Joe, excuse me—Karen was explaining her point of view about *x* when you started to respond. I'd like you to let her finish before you add your perspective." Joe knows exactly why you stopped him and what you'd like him to do differently. And you've pointed it out in a way that's neutral and behavioral—that doesn't make him the bad guy—so he also feels protected in the process. Remember, it's important that you be as respectful to the person who's forgotten the agreement as you're asking him or her to be to the rest of the group.

In other words, during this step you let people know in what way the agreement isn't being kept and what has to happen differently so that everyone can contribute fully. As the facilitator, when you use the "protect" skill, you're simply reminding people of the agreements they've made about how to work together well. You're the "respect and fairness safety net" for the group.

BACK TO DAVID AND ALLTEA

Let's look in again on David and the CTF. They've finished the "what is" step and also "what's the hope." They've created a clear vision of their hoped-for future (what it would look and feel like if HQ and the field offices were really communicating well and what the positive impact would be on employees and on results). And they did it all in one meeting. Now they've come back together for the next meeting, focusing on "what's in the way"—the obstacles to the vision. David started by reconfirming the "road rules" they created in the last meeting: what they agreed on was "listen before disagreeing," "no interrupting" (this is a passionate crowd), and "make 'real' agreements" (versus telling the group you agree, then speaking against the group's decision to others later). Here's what's happening now:

David's starting to realize this part of the process might present some problems—and he's really focusing on his protecting skills. It's clear to him that Dom is the sort of person who tends to super-size the obstacles and talk about them as though they're impossible to overcome, and that both Joan and Antwan are from the "see no evil" school—Joan because she doesn't want to everybody to get bummed out and Antwan because he just wants to move-it-along-and-solve-the-damn-problem-already. The task force is supposedly looking at obstacles inside the company, but it's rough going.

Elinor begins, "Well, one obstacle, I think, is that lots of people at headquarters have never worked in a field office, and so they don't know what's—"

Antwan interrupts, seeming impatient. "I don't think that's such a big deal, you know, Elinor. It's—"

David breaks in. "Hold up, Antwan. We're just getting everything on the table. Elinor?"

Elinor finishes her thought. "Just it's hard to communicate well about things you've never experienced. Sometimes when I talk to folks at HQ, I can tell you have no idea what I'm dealing with."

"OK, so 'lack of shared experience between field and HQ'?" David says as he writes.

"Yeah." Elinor nods.

Dom jumps in. "You know, I don't think there's anything to be done about that. I mean, what are you going to do, have everybody trade jobs for a week? I've never worked in a company where people understand each other's jobs. If we try to solve for that, we'll be here forever."

David puts up a hand. "Dom, we're just looking at the obstacles. We're not trying to solve them or figure out whether they're solvable. We're just naming them."

"Well, all right, then," Dom says. "I'd say an obstacle is some people's unrealistic expectations about communication. I mean, does anybody communicate well? Not in my life."

Joan responds, clearly uncomfortable, "Come on, Dom, if we listened to you, why would we even be on this team? You're making it sound like a lost cause—"

David breaks in again, gently. "Wait a sec, Joan, let's just note Dom's obstacle. 'Unrealistic expectations,'" he says as he writes. "Is that it, Dom?"

"Absolutely," Dom says.

"And thinking good communication is impossible—that's an obstacle, too," Joan adds.

"Fair enough," David says; he writes briefly, then turns back to the group. "OK, more obstacles?"

Now, I have to say, I've never had a group be this cantankerous when I was facilitating an obstacles discussion, but I'm making a point here. If you as the facilitator are consistent in protecting everyone's right to contribute, almost any potential wrangle can be averted, and the conversation can continue to move forward. The essence of the Protect skill is: *never take sides.* Remember, you as the facilitator are an advocate for fairness, honesty, and consensus rather than for a particular person, point of view, or solution. It's Fair Witnessing at its finest.

Keep on Track

Clarifying and protecting both help to create an environment where people feel free to be creative and to take risks and where misunderstanding and bad feeling are reduced to a minimum. They assure that all the group members' relevant knowledge, experience, and points of view are included in the conversation. The skill of *keeping on track* balances these first two by assuring that the group also accomplishes its goals.

The steps of this skill are very similar to those of protecting. One way of looking at it: here you're protecting the group's need to achieve certain results.

KEEP ON TRACK

- get agreement about the process
- notice where the group is, relative to the process
- say what you see/ask for what's needed

GET AGREEMENT ABOUT THE PROCESS: Again, you can't hold people responsible for something they haven't agreed to, so you need to agree up front—as a group—about what the process is and how you'll use it. These agreements should focus on *what*, *why*, and *how long*. You'll use your feedback skills of specificity to make these agreements.

Let's say, for example, that you were about to begin the "what's the path" step of the vision and strategy model. You would tell the group:

- **What:** You'd explain the process, as I've outlined it in the previous chapter (pp. 164–209), providing examples as appropriate and outlining how the step works.
- **Why:** You'd let people know the goal of the step—in this case, you might say something like, "The point of doing this part of the process is to first agree on those core directional efforts we believe will best take us from where are to where we want to go and then create the tactical plans to implement those strategies. That way, we'll have a complete and agreed-upon map for moving forward."
- **How long:** You'd give people a sense of how much time this part of the process will take. You might say something like, "We should be done with this part of the process by about two P.M.; we can lengthen or

shorten lunch as we need to in order to finish by then."

In order to make this step work, you—as the facilitator—have to be very familiar with and clear about the model or process you're going to use. That way, you'll be able to share with the group the three things I've outlined in the previous list (what, why, and how long), stating them clearly up front and getting the group's agreement. This gives you a powerful "stake in the ground"—a clear reference point to come back to when the group needs help to stay on track.

NOTICE WHERE THE GROUP IS, RELATIVE TO THE PROCESS: As I noted earlier, in order to recognize whether or not the group is staying on track relative to the process, you need to have that process firmly in mind—what's supposed to happen, why, and when—while facilitating the group's work. If the process is new to you or you don't feel entirely confident that you have it firmly in mind, you can note the essence of the process for yourself on a little "cheat sheet," or—better yet—you can put the essence of "what, why, and how long" on a flip chart for the group.

I'd also suggest that you keep the following question in mind as a kind of check for keeping on track: "Are we going to be able to accomplish what we've agreed to in the allotted time?" If the answer is "no," look for problems with the what, the why, or the how long:

- **"What" problems:** Have people stopped working the process as agreed upon, either getting caught in un-related discussions, working at the wrong level (that is, with the camera pulled too far back or focused in too close), or working a different part of the process?

- **"Why" problems:** Have people lost sight of what you're trying to accomplish—are they bringing in information or issues that won't lead you toward your goals, or are they recommending (explicitly or implicitly) another agenda?
- **"How long" problems:** Are people going into more detail than necessary? Is anyone rambling or monologuing? Is the group getting distracted (by bad feelings in the group, tiredness, confusion, outside priorities) and therefore slowing down?

Once you've noticed that the group is off track and looked to see what's causing it, you're ready to move to the final part of "keeping on track."

SAY WHAT YOU SEE/ASK FOR WHAT'S NEEDED: As in the skills of clarifying and protecting, you'll use feedback skills here to share your observations (Fair Witnessing yet again!) and ask for needed change in as specific, neutral, and timely a way as possible.

Let's say you observe that the group is going into more-than-necessary detail, so that the step is taking considerably longer than you've agreed to give it. You might respond by saying something like, "I notice that we're only about halfway through, and we were shooting to be done with this step by noon. In order to move this step a little faster, I'd like to ask that you focus more on summarizing, rather than including anecdotes and commentary. I'd also like your permission to break in when people are giving a lot of detail and ask them for the essence of their observation. Is that OK with everybody?" (Once they've agreed and are back on track, you can use your skills of listening to restate people's contributions succinctly and accurately.)

One great little tool for getting people back on track that I've used over the years is the "parking lot." Sometimes group members get into tangential conversations that are important but not relevant to the discussion at hand. When that happens, it's sometimes difficult for them to let go of the irrelevant conversation and come back to the agreed-upon topic. In those situations, I often post a blank flip chart on the wall, title it "Parking Lot," and write the essence of the off-track-but-important issue on the chart. Then I say something like, "How about if we use this page to capture topics or thoughts that we don't want to lose but that aren't directly related to our goal in this meeting? That way we won't forget them and we can decide at the end of the meeting how and when to come back to them." This almost invariably makes people OK with refocusing on the agreed-upon topic.

By consistently employing your "keep on track" skill while facilitating, you're helping assure that the team reaches the goal or goals they've set for themselves—it's the antidote to waste-of-time meetings. When a meeting is kept on track, it tends to feel and be purposeful and productive.

KEEPING THE CTF ON TRACK

David and the team made it through the "what's in the way" part of vision and strategy in one piece and with a good set of prioritized internal and external obstacles, thanks to David's skillful facilitation and the group's insights. They've come back together for the "What's the Path: Strategies" meeting, and David notes that the feeling in the room is positive, almost buoyant; they're starting to realize that they're going to have a coherent and substantive set of recommendations for the senior team, and they're feeling pleased with themselves. David has sent everybody an e-mail explaining the "what, why, and how long" for this meeting and then briefly resummarized at the beginning to make sure everyone's clear. Now they're deciding on strategies:

> *"I think one strategy needs to be about communication protocol," notes Sharita. "You know, agreements about what kinds of things will get communicated."*
>
> *David starts a "mind map" flip chart, writing "communication protocols" inside a circle in the center, and then draws a line out from the circle and writes "what gets communicated" on it. Turning back to the group, he says, "OK, what are some other key elements of this core directional effort?"*
>
> *Luis says, "Not only what but to whom—we need to have some clear sense of who should be included in various communications . . . now it's all over the map. Some people do 'reply all' to practically the whole company, and other people don't tell anybody anything—you have to pry it out of them!" While he's talking, David draws another line out from the circle and writes "to whom" on it.*
>
> *Elinor says, "Yeah, remember that guy who used to run sales in the Central Region? You know him, Sharita. That guy wouldn't tell his own mother if he was getting married." People laugh.*
>
> *Sharita nods. "You're not far off. I swear, I had to convince*

him to share the commission structure with his direct reports."

Joan adds, "Yeah, some people are just naturally close-mouthed. I once had a boss—"

David jumps in. "Whoa! Come back, come back, you guys. We're running pretty far afield here." They turn back to him, smiling a little self-consciously.

"Thanks, David," Antwan says. "OK, so we also have to have some agreements about when, right? Like some things are very time-sensitive, and need to be communicated right away, while other things can wait a little longer."

David draws another line and writes "time frames" on it.

Aaron says, "Yeah, I think we should make a rule that you have to have all financial reports in by the second of the month. I know people are supposed to get them in by the eighth, but that makes it hard to close the month in a timely way—"

Dom interrupts. "That's not realistic, Aaron—some departments don't even get their results till the first, and—"

David breaks in. "Hey, Aaron, can you hold that thought till later, when we get to the specific tactics? Maybe you can write it down, so you don't lose it." He turns to Dom. "And you can argue with him then." Dom actually grins.

David turns back to the group. "So, what do you think, are we ready to try framing this first strategy as a statement?"

As you can see, the skill of keeping on track—once you've made the initial agreements about what "on track" means—consists primarily of consistently and respectfully redirecting people's attention back to the matter at hand. Though it sounds simple, I've found this is an extraordinarily useful thing to be able to do. I bet if you asked everybody you know what they find most frustrating about the meetings they attend, most of them would cite some version of this tendency for meetings to get off track. Imagine what would have happened in the preceding meeting if there had been no David: they'd still be talking about all the people they know who are reluctant communicators! (And just so you're not left hanging, the AllTea team's first strategy ended up being "Determine simple company-wide communication protocols for 'what, who, and when.'")

AS PROMISED: CAMERA CHECK

Since each of the three facilitator skills involves some version of "say what you see," it's a perfect use of the feedback approach we call camera check. Here's how it works: when you want to give feedback to someone, imagine you have a video camera, recording the behavior that needs changing. Then play the "tape" in your head and notice what you see and hear the person doing. Give your feedback based on what's "on the tape."

For instance, a video camera wouldn't show someone being "aloof and uninvolved" at a meeting, but it would record the person not making eye contact, doing paperwork when others are talking, or not responding to invitations to contribute. These what-shows-up-on-the-tape things would be much easier to hear than "you're aloof and uninvolved," because, while not positive, these "camera check" observations are essentially neutral and non-judgmental. It's a perfect way to "say what you see." (Again, for a fuller explanation and an activity to help you practice this approach, you may want to look at chapter 7 of *Growing Great Employees*.)

TAKING IT BACK TO THE REAL WORLD

I think of my facilitation skills as a kind of always-available meeting first-aid kit, a set of things I know how to do that makes it much more likely that people will have a productive meeting that's also engaging and fun and that takes full advantage of everybody in the room. Skillful facilitation can improve any meeting, from the simplest weekly staff check-in to a full-blown two-day vision and strategy session. Figure 4 shows a simple way to visualize the skills:

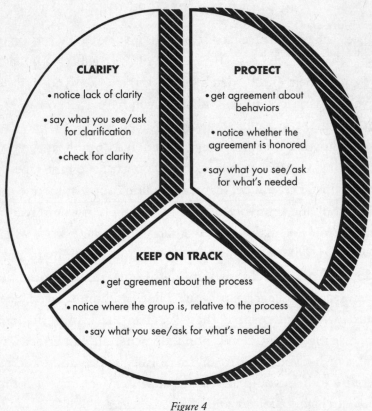

Figure 4

Try It Out

Since they're useful in nearly any meeting, I want to give you a chance to plan for taking these skills out for a test drive in a low-risk setting:

✓ Think of a meeting that fulfills the following criteria:

- It is reasonably simple and low-risk (that is, will be fairly brief, with participants who are neither very negative nor extremely high-level, and a straightforward agenda).
- You believe skillful facilitation would be helpful in this meeting.
- The other participants would accept your offer to facilitate. Note the particulars of the meeting below:

_____

_____

_____

_____

_____

_____

_____

Prepare to clarify: Review the section on the Clarify skill, then:

✓ Note below your own signs of lack of clarity—how will you know when you don't understand something?

_____

_____

_____

_____

_____

✓ How does this particular meeting tend to get unclear—e.g., do people ramble, do they get into "violent agreement," or do they use jargon or say obscure things?

_____

_____

_____

_____

_____

_____

✓ Given these probabilities, note some simple phrases you might use to "say what you see/ask for clarification."

_____

_____

_____

_____

_____

_____

Prepare to protect: Review the section on the Protect skill, then:

✓ How will you get agreement about behaviors? For instance, will you set ground rules that suit the particular process you're using (like brainstorming), or will you encourage the group to make their own "road rules" for the meeting? Summarize your approach below:

_____

_____

_____

_____

_____

✓ Given this group, note below what sorts of "not keeping the agreements" issues you think are most likely—e.g., interrupting, disagreeing before understanding, dismissing or invalidating people's ideas, etc.

_____

_____

_____

_____

_____

_____

_____

✓ Note some phrases you might use to "say what you see/ask for what's needed" when you need to "protect" in these cases. (Remember that your response needs to be equally respectful of the person you're protecting and the person from whom you're protecting him or her!)

_____

_____

_____

_____

_____

_____

_____

Prepare to keep on track: Review the section on the Keep on Track skill, then:

✓ Think about this meeting and the particular topics you'll be discussing. Note on the next page the three parts of the process for this meeting:

What: How will you explain the process you'll be using (e.g., brain-storming, problem-solving, open discussion, etc.)?

_____

_____

_____

_____

_____

_____

_____

Why: How will you explain the goal of the meeting (e.g., to share information, to come to a decision, to generate options, etc.)?

_____

_____

_____

_____

_____

_____

How long: How will you let the group know how much time they have for the process? (For instance, in a one-hour meeting, you might be taking twenty minutes to brainstorm, ten minutes to select feasible possibilities, and thirty minutes to agree on which one to pursue.)

_____

_____

_____

_____

_____

_____

✓ Note below which "getting off track" pitfalls this particular group is likely to fall into (e.g., going off on tangents, getting into too much detail, having conversations that are better had offline or with a smaller group):

_____

_____

_____

_____

_____

_____

_____

✓ Note some phrases you might use to "say what you see/ask for what's needed" in order to get the group back on track in these situations:

_____

_____

_____

_____

_____

_____

✓ Finally, note a self-talk statement you can employ to help yourself maintain the mind-set of a facilitator: that is, advocating for fairness, honesty, and consensus rather than for a particular person, point of view, or solution.

_____

_____

_____

_____

_____

_____

A LITTLE OR A LOT

Even if you doubt that you'll use this whole "facilitation tool kit" (you may not regularly run meetings or you may not feel you have the personal makeup to play this role with a group), even having little bits of these skills can come in very handy. For example, I'm much more likely to get good, clear agreements about "what, why, and how long" in one-on-one meetings as a result of having some understanding of facilitation skills. So, just let this chapter sink into your brain and bones and I suspect what you've learned here will support you in surprising ways.

In Real Life:

Look for places in your daily life to begin using both the skills and the mind-set of facilitation. For example, if you notice two colleagues in violent agreement, you might "say what you see/ask for clarification," as in, "Hey, Joe, I think you and Emily are actually saying kind of the same thing—it sounds like you're both concerned about the impact on sales. Is that it?"

FOURTEEN

Strategy as a Way of Life

Standing inside the tumbled walls that remain of Cricci-eth Castle, you can see it's a patchwork of different building styles and eras: some stones are larger, some smaller; some of the walls are thicker; in a few places the stone is more finely cut. There are even a few modern additions—the iron railing and the commentary under Plexiglas are definitely post–thirteenth century! The castle has clearly evolved throughout its history, and is still evolving today, in its role as a historic landmark and tourist spot.

Llewellyn may have built the core of the castle we see today, but historians believe there was probably a wooden fortification of some kind on the hill long before he was born—and the Norman kings who came after Llewellyn expanded and strengthened the castle he began, changing it to suit their own purposes.

This is all to remind you of something I've been saying through our conversation. Being strategic is not a onetime thing. You don't "build your castle on the hill" and then abandon it. As the current reality changes, and perhaps the hoped-for future as well, so change *those core directional choices* (and the tactics to implement them) *that will best move you toward your hoped-for future*. The consistent focus I've been referencing throughout is not a static unmoving focus but rather a "live" focus on the world and your hopes as they now exist.

In chapter 9, I talked about how to reposition your thinking in order to keep your focus fresh and accurate. You may want to go back and reread or skim that chapter; if not, here's the model as a quick reminder:

STRATEGIC REPOSITIONING

Refresh *What Is Now*

Reconfirm *the Hope*

Reassess *What's in the Way*

Revise *the Path*

Keeping your strategic focus alive and current is very much the same whether you're working by yourself or with others—in fact, you may remember that I used a group example in chapter 9, with Alicia and her team from greenbambino.com. The major difference is that with a group, it's more important to carve out and agree on specific times to devote to strategic conversations. When it's just you, you can decide to spend ten minutes, or two hours, to go through the repositioning process whenever you like; it's simply a matter of reminding yourself and finding the time. With a group, it's unlikely to "just happen." And so if you don't set aside time for being

248

strategic, "tactical entropy" will almost certainly take place—the group will drift back into a focus on firefighting, individual priorities, and turf wars and stop *consistently making those core directional choices*. . . .

You get the picture.

So, I want to share with you some ideas about how to help a group stay strategic both day-to-day and long-term. I invite you to play around, test them out, and find out what works for the group or groups you're supporting in their strategic focus.

STAYING STRATEGIC DAY TO DAY

I've discovered, over the years, that most groups need a "keeper of the flame" to support them in staying strategic on an ongoing basis. This is generally the person (you?) who is most aware of the possibility of staying strategic about the challenge and most motivated by the benefits of doing so. This person's awareness and motivation tend to continually respark the flame of others' awareness and motivation pretty naturally, but there are also some specific tools you can use to help keep that fire burning:

VISION CARDS: I encourage the use of this tool with most of the groups I support in being strategic. It's very simple: once you've agreed on the core elements of your hoped-for future, print them on a card, make a copy for everyone in the group, laminate them, and hand them out at a meeting, inviting everyone to put their card where they'll see it often—taped to their computer, in their wallet, propped on their in-box.

(These vision cards generally look very much like the examples I provided on pp. 188–189.) You can get a little fancy if you want and include your company logo or colors . . . but the important thing is the vision. Having a card like this keeps the vision—the desired outcome—in the forefront of people's minds.

"STRATEGY SCREENING": I've seen strategic leaders do this often, and I make every effort to do it with my clients and in my own company. "Strategy screening" simply means bringing your agreed-upon strategies into day-to-day conversation as a screen for action. Here's how this works. Let's say someone in the group comes up with an idea for a new initiative and is suggesting that resources be allocated toward it. You might ask, "How does that initiative support our strategies?" or, "Which of our strategies do you see that initiative as supporting?" This will help remind everyone to use the strategies as a guide in making decisions about how to use your time and resources.

TACTICAL CHECK-INS: Interestingly, one way to keep the group strategic is to hold them accountable for achieving the tactics to which they've committed in vision and strategy. It reinforces the through-line from vision through strategy to tactical execution and reminds people that being *truly* strategic is a very practical approach. Otherwise, when people make specific commitments in a vision and strategy session and then don't keep these commitments, they end up feeling that being strategic isn't "real." They tend to drift back into reacting to whatever comes over the transom on a given day and lose sight of their hoped-for future. A great way to do effective tactical check-ins is to append them to already-existing meetings. So, for instance, if Alicia at greenbambino.com has a weekly staff meeting, she might have everyone pull out their strategic plan document at the end of every other meeting and spend fifteen minutes checking on progress, discussing and dealing with obstacles, and making any needed "tweaks" in order to keep moving forward. That way, they're assessing their progress toward the vision at least a couple of times a month and it begins to feel like a normal part of doing business.

COMMON LANGUAGE: I've noticed that leaders who are committed to keeping the strategic approach alive often make the effort to include words, phrases, and concepts from their vision and strategy in their day-to-day conversations with people. For instance, one of our client groups has as two of their vision elements "New Frontiers" (by which they mean finding and exploring new revenue streams) and "Brand in Demand" (a reminder that part of their vision is to support and leverage their company's brands). I recently heard the head of the division say to his team in a meeting, when talking about a new business opportunity that involved extending one of the existing brands, "I love that—it's Brand in Demand in the New Frontier!" Everybody laughed, but they knew what he meant, and they all saw that the initiative they were talking about was fully directionally correct.

BEING STRATEGIC FOR THE LONG HAUL

These small but powerful daily or weekly reminders will definitely keep your group headed in the right direction. And I've also found that at some point it's important to pull everyone out of the fray and really look at your plan in depth, to do focused vision and strategy review meetings.

There's a kind of natural "1, 2" cadence to this, I've found. It's generally very helpful to do a first "repositioning" four to six months after the initial session and then to do what I think of as a "full reboot" twelve to eighteen months after the initial session. Each one serves an important purpose in keeping the group focused and in keeping the vision and strategy alive and relevant.

Four- to Six-Month Repositioning

This seems to work well as a six-hour (or so) meeting. You follow the steps of the model on p. 248, first looking to see if there are significant changes in your current reality and then reaffirming your mission (if that was part of your original session), your vision, and your strategies. This usually goes pretty quickly, as those things are unlikely to have changed in this relatively brief period. You also look to see whether any major new obstacles have arisen,

Then you go through each strategy and its tactics one at a time, noting which tactics have been completed and which haven't. For the ones that have been completed, you note whether they yielded the results you were looking for or there are additional steps you may have to take. For the tactics that haven't been completed, you focus on understanding what got in the way. It's important to note that this is a learning conversation, not an assessing-blame conversation. You're not trying to figure out who screwed up—you're simply trying to figure out how to improve, as a group, going forward. Once you have a clear understanding of what impeded you in a particular tactic, you can decide whether you want to (1) re-commit to it (and how you'll overcome what stopped you before), (2) agree on a different way of achieving the same result, or (3) let it go (you may well have decided that it's not worth the effort it will require, or you may now see that you didn't do it the first time because it wasn't as important as you had originally thought!).

Once you've agreed upon your renewed tactical plan, make sure that you've clarified the what, who, and when to everyone's satisfaction. Also clarify how you'll continue to stay in touch and hold yourselves accountable going forward. (If the ways you've used till now are working, you can simply acknowledge that and recommit to them; if not, you may want to explore why and craft new, more doable ways to stay focused on your vision and strategy.)

It seems that four to six months is a good time frame for this initial repositioning for two reasons: first, it gives the group enough time to get some traction and see some results—so there's often a nice celebratory aspect to the meeting—and second, it's very often toward the end of the initial "tactical cycle." You may remember that when I was first explaining strategy and tactics I talked about the appropriate time frames for both strategy and tactics and noted that it usually makes the best sense to create tactical plans for the next four to eight months. If you have the repositioning meeting at the four- to six-month mark, it will usually mean you're ready to create the next "set" of tactics to implement your strategies.

Twelve- to Eighteen-Month Reboot

This meeting is a chance to do a full review of your entire strategic vision. In the year to year and a half since you did your initial session, a lot will have happened. If the group has stayed reasonably focused, you will have had a chance to see whether your vision (and mission, if you've created one) truly represent your hoped-for future relative to the challenge you've identified. You'll also probably be at or near the end of your initial "strategic cycle" (you may recall that I noted twelve to eighteen months as an appropriate time frame for strategy).

I've found it's good to allow a full day for this meeting—or even a day and a half, if there have been lots of changes—and go through all the steps of the model in depth:

- **Refresh the *What Is Now*:** First, do a thorough update of your current state, noting what has changed and what's stayed the same. You can build from your initial SWOT analysis, or you may even want to start fresh and redo the SWOT completely and then compare it to the original one, to see how both your perspective and the situation have changed.
- **Reconfirm *the Hope*:** Review your mission, if you've created one. Does it still seem like the best expression of your purpose? (In my experience, mission

seldom changes over this period of time, but you and your group may have gotten a clearer sense of what your mission actually is and may decide to revise your mission statement as a result of this increased clarity.)

Now, look at your vision elements. Are they still the "bones" of your hoped-for future, or is something missing? For example, when my company, Proteus, did this "reboot" after our first vision and strategy session, we realized that our vision focused on the professional environment we wanted to create for ourselves and the experience and results we wanted to offer our clients, but that it didn't clearly describe how we wanted to grow. We added a vision element that we called Strategic Zeros—meaning that we want to increase our revenues (add zeros onto the end of our total income figure), but only in ways that support our vision and strategy and are fully aligned with the kind of organization we want to be.

You might "subtract" elements, rather than add them. You might agree that one element is less important than the others and decide to remove it. Or perhaps you realize that two elements can be combined. One of our client companies initially had two vision elements, "Balanced, Happy Team" and "Strategic Efficiencies." During their "reboot," they came to feel those two things were really parts of a single aspect of their hope and combined these elements into "Capitalizing on Our Great Team." This is your chance to take advantage of all the clarity you've gained over the past twelve to eighteen months about your true hope and to massage your vision to make it even more resonant and compelling.

- **Reassess *What's in the Way:*** This part of the process can provide important learning. I recommend you first review your initial assessment of the obstacles—the internal and external obstacles that, in your original session, you believed would be the most important to address—and see how accurate you were. People are often surprised to realize that obstacles they thought would present the greatest difficulty were relatively easy to overcome, while others they overlooked or assumed would be minor were much more problematic. One client group had assumed their biggest internal obstacle would be to get buy-in for their vision at the senior levels of the company. As it turned out, senior management actually embraced their vision and strategy and were very complimentary about the clarity and depth of their plan. The biggest actual internal obstacle (which they hadn't even mentioned the first time around) ended up being resistance to the plan on the part of some longtime employees within the department.

  Once you've done this learning-focused review, work together to create an updated, more accurate picture of the key internal and external obstacles to your success.

- ***Revise the Path—Strategies:*** Now it's time to redraw your path: to create strategies and tactics that will take you from where you are now to where you now want to go. You may find that one or more of your strategies are still essential and that you simply need to create a new set of tactics for continuing to implement them. For instance, one of our media clients had as an initial strategy "create and implement an effective organizational structure that includes people, systems, and processes." A year later, during their reboot, they agreed they were still right in the thick of doing that and definitely needed to leave it in the plan and keep working toward it.

However, you may have completed one strategy and be ready to create a new strategy that builds on that success. This same media company had as one of its original strategies "create an ongoing, interactive mechanism for understanding our audiences." At the reboot session, they agreed that had been completed (and was working very well). What they decided they needed to do at this new point in their evolution was "institutionalize quick, effective ways to respond to what our audience is telling us."

Finally, you may need to create entirely new strategies, given the change in your circumstances or the work you've done to date. For instance, when my first book was published at the end of 2006, my colleagues and I at Proteus realized we needed to create a new strategy focused on capturing the business benefits of that major change in our current reality.

- **_Revise the Path—Tactics:_** Once you've revised your strategies, you can work together to create new tactical plans that will allow you to implement them.

Review the tactics from your first twelve to eighteen months to get clearer about what worked and what didn't, so that the tactics you agree on in this iteration are even more likely to bear fruit. As you review, you're likely to see useful patterns: many of our clients note that they routinely get tripped up by a few common planning problems. When they factor these things into their planning, they're much more successful at achieving what they set out to do. Here's a little "bonus insight" to help you in defining your group's Achilles' heels in tactical planning:

The Top Five Mistakes in Action Planning:

- underestimating time and complexity of execution
- not fully factoring in current commitments
- not anticipating system implications, effects, and pushbacks
- not looking at execution through the eyes of those doing the work
- underestimating needed communication and coordination

WHY IT'S GOOD

The real beauty of taking the time and energy to do an in-depth reboot like this is that pretty much everyone in the group will start to feel the momentum of the approach, the power of being strategic. Any lingering thought that this is simply an intellectual exercise, one that doesn't support real success, will begin to evaporate. It's like the "flywheel" effect that Jim Collins talks about in *Good to Great:* the process will begin to take on a life of its own and require less and less "above and beyond" attention to keep going.

You and your group will be well on your way to being strategic.

In Real Life:

You can experiment with helping groups be day-to-day strategic in smaller ways, as well. For instance, in meetings of any group of which you're a member, you can encourage reviewing the current reality or the obstacles—especially when things have changed. You might say something like, "What's changed since we last met?" or, "Anything new we need to watch out for?" You can also bring the group back to a focus on desired outcomes, by asking questions like, "Will this help us achieve our goals?" or, "How does that move us toward what we're trying to accomplish?"

FIFTEEN

Castle Building for Fun and Profit

I'm sure it won't surprise you to know that I feel a real connection to Wales and to Criccieth and Llewellyn especially. I love that Llewellyn envisioned a united Wales and that he spent years making that happen and keeping it together. He died in his sixties—a good, long life by thirteenth-century standards—in his bed at Aberconwy and still the Prince of North Wales. It seems to me that he was clear about his purpose and *consistently made those core directional choices that would* . . .

As I write this, I'm sitting cross-legged on the deck of my long-envisioned dream house, tapping away on my laptop. It's a gorgeous fall day in the Hudson Valley, full of the honey-colored light that lies long across the hills this time of year. The trees are glowing in patches of vermilion and pumpkin orange and deep yellow, and I can see beyond the river spread out below me, all the way to Connecticut. After years of planning and effort, I'm living here. I did it. I feel a kinship with Llewellyn. Having actually created my own castle on the hill, I feel capable of much more.

One of the great things about being strategic is that it's self-reinforcing. When you actually achieve an important part of your hoped-for future by staying focused on the efforts that will get you there, it's a wonderful, powerful feeling. You have a practical experience of your own potential. You want to keep doing it.

I want you to experience that. It would make me very sad if you went all the way through this book with me and then somehow didn't take advantage of what's been offered here.

So, in this last chapter, I'd like to help you be strategic about being strategic. (And if I've finally gone over the line and that last sentence is just too much, I'll say it differently: I just want to increase the odds you'll be able to use this stuff.)

ENCOURAGING YOURSELF

Incorporating new approaches or behaviors into your life (or not) often depends on how you talk to yourself about them. Let's apply what you've learned about self-talk to the challenge of fully integrating the art of being strategic into your life. Just to remind you, here's the model for managing your self-talk:

———————— **MANAGING YOUR SELF-TALK** ————————

Recognize

Record

Revise

Repeat

I suggest you start by looking at what you're saying to yourself about being strategic. Your self-talk may be positive and supportive, which would be great: you might be telling yourself you're excited about using this approach or that you feel capable of thinking and acting in this way. If that's what you're thinking, rock on.

However, if your self-talk is less hopeful and positive—and you actually do want to apply the principles and approaches in this book—you can use this model to change your interior monologue.

Let's say, for instance, that you're saying to yourself, *I can't do this because I'm___*. Fill in the blank: your own self-sabotaging rationale could be just about anything: *not a leader,* for instance, or *too busy,* or, *just not very good at long-term thinking.* As soon as you become aware of whatever your negative self-talk is, you'll write it down. Let's say, for purposes of this example, that it's, *I can't do this, because I'm just not very good at long-term thinking.*

Then you'll read what you've written and, in your Fair Witness mode, ask yourself what impact it has on you to think this way. If you were saying the preceding sentence to yourself, I suspect it would make you feel demoralized and frustrated. You might simply put the book away and forget about it. It's not much fun to think about something if you believe you're not capable of doing it.

So, having understood the negative, counterproductive impact this self-talk is having on you, you'd revise it. You'd ask yourself: *What could I say to myself instead, that I would believe and that would support me in learning and using these skills and this approach?* Perhaps your revised self-talk might be, *I've not done much long-term thinking in the past, but that doesn't mean I'm not capable of it. And I'd like to learn. Or, I understand this approach, and I've used it already in the exercises in the book. I don't have any reason to believe I won't keep being able to apply it.*

Then, any time your former I-can't-do-this self-talk rears its ugly head, you'll use your revised, more accurate self-talk to coach yourself toward success.

Try It: Managing Your Self-Talk

Now I invite you to try the model, using any actual negative self-talk you may be having about your own ability to benefit from using this process.

✓ Recognize something you're saying to yourself about being strategic that's counterproductive. Record it below:

✓ Note below the negative impact you believe this self-talk is having or might have on how you feel or act:

✓ Revise it by writing new self-talk that you could use in this situation—remember, craft self-talk that you believe and that will have a more positive impact:

✓ Finally, note a few ideas for "repeating"—for making this rethought self-talk a new mental habit as you continue to explore being strategic:

ENGAGING YOUR PASSION

In chapter 11, I talked about how to invite others into the process of being strategic by increasing their *awareness*—helping them see that they could approach the situation in this way—and their *motivation*—helping them see the personal benefit in doing so. It's no different for you: awareness and motivation are equally central to your own learning! I'm assuming that, having made it this far in the book, you're well aware that you *could* approach your life more strategically. The question is, are you motivated to do so?

So, let's do a little brainstorm. In the space below, write down all the situations and endeavors in your life that are important to you. Don't think too much about it, just write them down:

Now, circle those areas in the box that you feel would benefit most from being approached more strategically. In other words, where would it be most helpful to get clearer about your hoped-for future and the core choices you'll need to make to achieve those outcomes? Once you've decided, I suggest you take yourself through the following activity.

Try It: Finding Your Motivation

✓ Select one of the areas you have chosen in the box on page 265 where you feel it would be beneficial to be more strategic, and summarize it below:

✓ Note below the benefits you might gain from approaching this situation or endeavor more strategically:

✓ Why are those benefits important to you?

That's it. As I said earlier, if someone has awareness and motivation, then he or she is generally ready to learn and then to behave differently. And, once you have understood your own motivation, you can reengage it by reminding yourself of the personal benefits of using this (or any) approach when your attention or commitment begins to flag.

NOTING THE REWARDS

Just as an added support for your motivation, I'd like you to think about any ways in which being more strategic has helped you already. I've noticed that people are sometimes surprised to realize that a new idea or approach has already benefited them, even before they've "tried" to use it. As you've read this book, have you started to think or act in ways that serve you better? If so, note them below:

The more you recognize the rewards—both intrinsic and extrinsic—you can gain from being strategic, the more likely you are to continue using the approach. As long as we're on the "rewards" conversation, let's look back in on David Chen and the group at AllTea, just to see what happened. . . .

The CTF has just finished its final presentation to the CEO and the rest of the senior team, and it went very well. The senior team was impressed by the clarity and specificity of their recommendations, and the CEO noted that she and the senior team would be spending their next monthly staff meeting figuring out how best to implement the recommendations. Then the CEO smiled at them and assured them that when she shared the recommendations at the all-company Town Hall next month, Dave, Joan, and the team would be getting all the credit.

Everyone on the CTF was jazzed at the response they'd gotten and, on the spur of the moment, they decided to have dinner together by way of celebration.

They've all settled in around their table at a cozy neighborhood Mexican restaurant—festive, but quiet enough for talking—and have ordered drinks and nachos.

"You know," Dom says reflectively to Dave, "I really thought this whole being-strategic thing was a crock when you first started talking about it."

Antwan widens his eyes in mock surprise. "No. Really?" he says, and everybody laughs.

Dom waves away the interruption. "Yeah, yeah, you're funny. Anyway, this stuff works OK." He raises his mojito in Dave's direction. "Thanks."

"Hear, hear," adds Joan. "You saved my butt, Dave. There's no way we would have gotten here without you and your 'being-strategic' thing."

Everyone murmurs agreement and raises their glass. Dave, slightly abashed, thanks them all. "And I have other good news, as well," he says. "My boss is leaving for a bigger job in the industry—and the CEO pulled me aside after the meeting today and said they'd like to offer me his job."

"Dave, that's great!" Joan says, and the rest of the team add their congratulations, with Sharita patting him on the shoulder from one side and Elinor giving him a one-armed hug from the other.

"Well," says Luis, "here's what I think. Now that I actually know what it means to be strategic, and everybody seems to live happily ever after as a result of doing it, maybe I'll give it a try in Customer Relations. . . ."

I love it when clients of ours start to benefit from being more strategic. Confusion and frustration go down; people start seeing the possibilities and getting excited about them; teams start working together more effectively and focusing better on what's most important. I would say that it's my very favorite professional experience when a client—an individual or an organization—starts getting clear about and then moving toward their hoped-for future.

It's what I hope for you. Thank you for giving me the opportunity to spend this time with you; may your life and your work be what you want them to be.

In Real Life:

When I coach an executive, we work together to agree on words or phrases for a reminder card, focused on what he or she wants to do differently and why. After the session, my assistant at Proteus creates a laminated version and sends it to the executive, who keeps it close at hand—on her computer, or in his wallet, or wherever it will be easy to see and remember.

Though I can't do that for you, I'd like to encourage you to create one for yourself and keep it where it will remind you of your intention.

In the box opposite (or on another page, if you actually want to laminate it), write a phrase or sentence that will remind you of why you want to be more strategic.

Proteus International

If you've enjoyed this book and found it helpful, I'd like to invite you to further explore the work we do at Proteus International. Some of it is directly related to what you've read here; as I've mentioned throughout the book, we work with a wide variety of groups and companies to help them craft clear vision and strategy for their enterprises—to help them clarify and move toward their hoped-for future.

In addition, my colleagues and I coach executives one-on-one to support them in creating the careers and lives they want, using many of the approaches I've shared with you here. We also offer group seminars to help participants develop the skills of being strategic, as well as a variety of other management and leadership skills.

If you'd like to find out more about the work we do and how it might benefit you or your organization, please feel free to explore our Web site, at www.proteus-international .com, or to contact us at connect@proteus-international .com.

Thank you once again for your time, your attention, and your curiosity!